Pan-African Psychologies

Series Editors

Chalmer E. F. Thompson
Indiana University – Purdue University Indianapolis
Indianapolis, IN, USA

Guerda Nicolas
University of Miami
Coral Gables, FL, USA

African people and their descendants from various regions of the Diaspora have endured a history of struggle that has been replete in violence and structural oppression. Offering a *psychology* of Black people entails an understanding of these pervasive, sustaining structures and their intersection with culture, gender socialization, and the panoply of "isms" that shape people and contexts. What is needed as part of a knowledge base on Black psychology is an elaboration of the common themes that cut across global contexts and the conditions that characterize specific regions, all of which have bearing on individual, interpersonal, and societal functioning. More than ever, there is an urgent need for psychological scholarship that unapologetically centers race and the ever-changing role of context in understanding the history, struggles, and strengths of Black lives and communities around the globe. The series seeks to make a novel contribution to the broader area of critical & radical psychology by drawing on marginalized voices and perspectives and by engaging with the praxis agenda of improving the lives of African/Black peoples. It both seeks to critique oppression (more particularly, of the racialized, neo-colonial world) and provide prospective strategies (practices of liberation, of peace) to respond to such forms of oppression.

Ismahan Soukeyna Diop

Adornment, Masquerade and African Femininity

palgrave
macmillan

Ismahan Soukeyna Diop
Department of Psychology
Cheikh Anta Diop University, Faculty
of Human and Social Sciences
Dakar, Senegal

ISSN 2523-8264 ISSN 2523-8272 (electronic)
Pan-African Psychologies
ISBN 978-3-031-28747-3 ISBN 978-3-031-28748-0 (eBook)
https://doi.org/10.1007/978-3-031-28748-0

Cover illustration: Ilene Perlman / Alamy Stock Photo

This Palgrave Macmillan imprint is published by the registered company Springer Nature Switzerland AG.
The registered company address is: Gewerbestrasse 11, 6330 Cham, Switzerland

Foreword

Ismahan Diop's voice as a Senegalese practicing analyst and scholar is essential to the canon of psychoanalytic literature. She writes with impressive clarity about the myths and traditions that give shape to our understanding of African femininity. Her focus hones even more specifically in on African women's adornment and the masquerade or "dance" they perform in their communities to negotiate cultural tradition, male patriarchy, and imperialism. Diop shares with readers the myths and traditions that inform African women's relationships with their families, husbands, children, and non-familial women that, combined, convey their expectations on how women *ought* to be. These collective aspects of their lives shape an understanding of their humanity as women and as members of their respective societies, and yet relatively little is written about them in the psychoanalytic literature. Speaking in the first-person plural and therefore signaling a cacophony of absented African-descended women, Diop writes: "We have chosen to actively participate in the development of this discipline in Africa because we believe that African cultural concepts must be used to resolve issues and promote transmission in society" (Chap. 1). Diop shares cultural and sociopolitical knowledge that reflects a reverence for ancestry, considered one of the key ingredients in confronting the ongoing misery and moral injury of people whose lives continue to be affected by violence and injustice (Connolly et al., 2022). In the book,

Diop also shares findings from her recent interviews with African women, includes thoughtful analyses of recent trends in their physical appearance, and concludes with richly descriptive case studies that incorporate psychoanalytic concepts and cultural/sociopolitical knowledge.

Diop's use of psychoanalytic concepts is not without controversy in view of Freud's views about non-European people as "primitive," which the author acknowledges. Indeed, Freud's psychoanalytic theory has been vigorously critiqued and contested by feminist and post-colonial scholars worldwide. His formulations have been outwardly rejected by many practitioners. Frantz Fanon (1952) famously took aim at the theory, calling it a colonizing tool that guides distressed people into adapting to the normativity of racism and societal repression rather than helping them sternly and wisely push against these forces (see also Hook & Truscott, 2018). Meanwhile, and over the span of more than a generation, scholars of psychology and psychiatry have continued to devise iterations of Freud's theory from his earliest formulations to his later developments, and with the expressed objectives of explaining patterns of disordered thinking, dysfunctional behaviors, and mood complaints associated with myriad diagnoses and with the individual complaints of depressive and anxious feelings.

Diop stays true to her commitment to use African concepts to explain and resolve the problems of African women. She does not engage in a comparative study in which African women's lives are examined and then scrutinized to fit European conceptions of "womanhood" as advanced by earlier Western and Western-influenced works. Nor does she downplay or ignore similarities that occur between traditions in her native Wolof society, on which she focuses, and traditions in other parts of the world. What she offers instead is an insightful review of how central psychoanalytic concepts, like the unconscious, symbols and lore that are suggestive of women's containment of power in societies alongside men's relative freedom toward powerful positions, and sexuality have relevance to Wolof society. Diop offers analyses of time-worn African tales and rituals with explanations to help identify the ambiguities that prevent African girls and women from *thriving* psychologically. Diop's careful contemplation provides a frame from which to help African women break from the contradictions and live healthier lives.

The author's work is reminiscent of a process that Parker and Pavón-Cuéllar (2002) call a revolution, both individually focused as a therapeutic approach and emancipatory as conceptualized as a pathway to the needed, emancipatory societal transformation. In their manifesto *Psychoanalysis and Revolution*, the authors contend that Freud's collection of writings is often miscast as universal in its application to understanding people. They state that Freud did not accept psychology as something given, real and entirely manifest, as something that could be known objectively, "nor did he see it as something unitary that would always be the self-same and same in every person" (p. 2). Parker and Pavón-Cuéllar also identified trends in how the earlier psychoanalytic writers and practitioners oriented themselves toward a sole adaptation model rather than one that combined individual transformation with societal advancement.

Diop provides a "clinical and political critique of misery" (Parker & Pavón-Cuéllar, 2002) that is consistent with an individual-and-societal transformation model. She begins with femininity, an expression of how women are taught and expected to be and behave in society. African women's femininity is shaped to perpetuate men's power and absorbed into cultural practices that simultaneously infantilize men (see Adichie, 2017) and aligns women into competitions with other women. Adornment of women's bodies is a feature of feminine expression, of the dance or masquerade, through myths and symbols of the suffering mother, the devouring mother, the spiteful and evil seducer, and the emasculating warrior. None of these symbols serve women well. As Diop notes, the role of women to contain their omnipotence for the sake of preserving men's dominance "does not leave much space for individual and professional accomplishment" (Chap. 2). The woman can be locked into a bind that is hardly between equals; men maintain their position as all-powerful. It is a masquerade that is played out in rites and rituals, in marriage ceremonies, and in "appropriate" interactions between men and women and with their families.

Still, how does psychoanalysis help the masses of people individually or collectively? Such a question is posed by South African scholars Kadish and Smith (2020) as well as "How do we address the ethical issues of health disparity and barriers to access of psychoanalytically oriented psychotherapy?" One way is to deepen one's concern for the violence that women experience all over the world. Psychoanalytic theory pushes us to think about maleness and masculinity, about men's overwhelming show of violence that targets women, human trafficking mostly of women, and the constricted, economic freedom of women that complicates their lives in an increasingly consumerist and oligarch-controlled world. This concern is decidedly a moral one.

As a woman born and raised in the US and whose African descendants were stolen from their land generations ago and sold into slavery, as I read Dr Diop's book, I found myself reflecting on the words by late anthropologist and author Zora Neale Hurston who described Black women in one of her novels as the mules of the world (Hurston, 1937). The United Nations, as one source, has provided documentation of the various abuses of African-descended women in different regions around the globe (United Nations Human Rights [UNHR], 2018). I cite as a more specific example the toll of the historic pandemic that begin in 2020 on the lives of Black American women in the US. I refer to the US because it is the context with which I am most familiar, and because it is a nation which many people outside of it believe to be comprised primarily of wealthy people.[1]

A 2020 *Essence* magazine study of Black American women reported that 64% of those surveyed agreed that the pandemic influenced their emotional well-being, while 63% reported that it influenced their mental health. Reports noted that Black Americans in general tend to get sicker and to live shorter lives with diseases (Williams et al., 2016) and that the spread of COVID-19 affirmed this trend. Battle and Carty (2022) report that women of color were distinctly impacted by the pandemic because of "the interconnected and compounded racial/ethnic inequities and gender inequities heightened by unemployment and low-wage employment, caregiving burdens, and unexpected consequences during the COVID-10 pandemic given the combination of stress and isolation from outside support systems." Unexpected consequences include a reported

[1] According to the Economic Policy Institute, in 2019, Black women were paid 33% less than their White male counterparts, which was a much larger gap than that between Black women and White women (25.7%) and Black men (22.2%) (Wilson, 2020). Among all racial group categories, which includes Whites, Blacks, and Latino/as, Black men and women wage earners have the highest rate of unemployment (EPI, 2022). Among all people residing in the US, the gap between the majority of workers and the very wealthy, often referred to as the 1%, has steadily risen for most of the last forty years or so (Gould & Kandra, 2022).

increase by the Centers for Disease Control and Prevention of intimate partner violence, which disproportionately affects women's safety over men (see Battle and Carty, 2022).

According to the Poor People's Campaign (PPC), women overall make up more than 75% of healthcare workers, almost 80% of frontline social workers, and more than 70% of government and community-based service workers (Poor People's Campaign [PPC] Pandemic Report, 2022). Based on my own observations anecdotally, the disproportionate presence of African-descended women in low-wage, essential care jobs is clearly noticeable in large US cities. Many are Afro-American as well as descendants from other countries, including countries in the Caribbean and Africa. In a half dozen or more senior citizens' facilities I have visited in my own community of Indianapolis, roughly 90–100% of the certified nursing assistants or CNAs are African-descended women.

The PPC reports that US public policy makers have consistently failed workers in general, but especially low-wage, frontline workers who were deemed essential in the early days of the pandemic. They continue:

> Many of these workers are still employed in jobs that fail to pay a living wage, work in unsafe and unhealthy working conditions, and have inadequate or non-existent worker benefits like health insurance, paid sick leave, and hazard pay. Black, Indigenous, Latinx, and other racially marginalized communities have shouldered a disproportionate burden at every phase of the pandemic due to the longstanding histories of structural, institutional, and systemic racism and other forms of structural violence experienced by these communities. Since the beginning of the pandemic, these groups have experienced *higher rates of severe illness and have died at higher rates and younger ages*, trends that cannot be solely attributed to vaccine inequities or underlying chronic conditions. (emphasis added)

As of 2022, twenty-two million jobs have been lost to COVID-19, and over 710,000 people have died in the US alone (PPC, 2022).

In the US and elsewhere around the world, African-descended women can be treated like mules—as lowly, expendable, exoticized, and underappreciated in our societies. We also have risen above these forces, affirmed by the UNHR (2020) report which chronicles both challenges and achievements, yet the expertise of mental health professionals whose interventions include measures to address the condemning structures is desperately needed. With the help of professional, civic, religious, and advocacy organizations whose members and constituencies take misery seriously, *all* people can encourage liberation from the strictures that prevent us from improving our health. The PPC is a multi-racial/ethnic organization that aims to get to the root of poverty in the US and does so by attuning itself to the various identity groups that are affected by class exploitation. Such political action arises from a concern for those in misery and is a useful template for regional and transnational advocacy. A psychology intent on invoking change in individuals as it also promotes societal change is a discipline committed to the improvement of African-descended people's lives (e.g., Kessi et al., 2021; Martín-Baró, 1996).

Emancipation is key to Diop's objective in writing this book. She masterfully interprets the rites, rituals, and symbols that constitute the socialization of girls and women in Wolof society and that have meaning to their daily lives as students, mothers, partners, and sisters to other women. Through her analyses and descriptions, she shows how she can act as a powerful catalyst to the women who seek her help by settling the contradictions they have adopted as they also struggle for cultural inclusion and belonging. It is a struggle that ultimately requires the efforts of many, akin to the PPC, and one which entails actions that both honor traditions with reverence and simultaneously promote shifts in cultural-sociopolitical milieus that have proven unhealthy. This book has the force to compel practicing psychologists who have even a sliver of interest in psychoanalysis to dip (further) into these theoretical waters to take part in the transformation of African women's lives. We need not toss away any conceptualization whose aim is to expose ambiguities and contradictions and thus to seek out ways to end them and liberate ourselves in the process.

Indiana University–Purdue University Indianapolis (IUPUI)
Indianapolis, IN, USA

Chalmer E. F. Thompson

References

Adichie, C. N. (2015). *We should all be feminists.* Anchor.

Battle, S., & Carty, D. (2022, October 6). Gendered racism among women of color. Retrieved from the U.S. Centers for Disease Control and Prevention website: https://blogs.cdc.gov/healthequity/2022/10/06/gendered-racism-among-women-of-color/

Connolly, M., Gobodo-Madikizela, P., Layton, L., Nichols, B., Pivnick, B., & Reading, R. (2022). What's repaired in reparations: A conversation among psychoanalytic and social activists. *Psychoanalytic Dialogues, 32*(1), 3–16. https://doi.org/proxy.ulib.uits.iu.edu/10.1080/10481885.2021.2013691

Economic Policy Institute [EPI], *State of Working America Data Library* (2022, December). Unemployment by gender and race. Retrieved from https://www.epi.org/data/#/?subject=unemp&g=*&r=*

Essence Magazine (2020, December 6). ESSENCE Releases 'Impact of COVID-19 on Black Women' Study. Retrieved from https://www.essence.com/health-and-wellness/essence-covid-19-black-women-study/

Fanon, F. (1952/1980). *Black skin, white masks.* Grove.

Gould, E., & Kandra, J. (2022, December 21). Inequality in annual earnings worsens in 2021. Retrieved from the Economic Policy Institute website. https://www.epi.org/publication/inequality-2021-ssa-data/

Hook, D., & Truscott, R. (2013). Fanonian ambivalence: On psychoanalysis and postcolonial critique. *Journal of Theoretical and Philosophical Psychology, 33*(2), 1555–169.

Hurston, Z. N. (1937). *Their eyes were watching God.* J. B. Lippincott.

Kadish, Y., & Smith, C. (2020). Psychoanalysis and psychoanalytic psychotherapy in the South African context. *Psychoanalytic Psychotherapy, 34*(2), 163–179.

Kessi, S., Boonzaier, F., & Gekeler, B. S. (2021). *Pan-Africanism and psychology in decolonial times.* Palgrave Macmillan.

Martín-Baró, I. (1996). *Writings for a liberation psychology.* Harvard University.

Parker, I., & Pavón-Cuéllar, D. (2021). *Psychoanalysis and revolution: Critical psychology for revolution movements.* 1968 Press.

Poor People's Campaign (2022, April). Poor people's campaign: A national call or moral revival. Pandemic Report. Retrieved from the PPC-NCMR website: https://www.poorpeoplescampaign.org/pandemic-report/

United Nations Human Rights (UNHR). (2020, January 15). Women and girls of African descent: Human rights achievements and challenges. UNHR Office of the High Commissioner, Geneva. Retrieved from https://www.

ohchr.org/en/documents/tools-and-resources/women-and-girls-african-descent-human-rights-achievements-and

Williams, D. R., Priest, N., & Anderson, N. B. (2016). Understanding associations among race, socioeconomic status, and health: Patterns and prospects. *Health Psychology, 35*(4), 407–411.

Wilson, V. (2020, November 21). Racism and the economy: Focus on employment. Retrieved from https://www.epi.org/blog/racism-and-the-economy-fed/

Acknowledgments

I would like to thank my family, especially my sisters and my parents, for their trust, support, and laughter. You are my source of inspiration. I would not be who I am today without your fabulous personalities.

To my friends. You are my strength, and I hope that you will be proud of this work.

To my colleagues. I am so glad to be part of this vibrant community. I would like to add a very special acknowledgment to Boubacar Barry, Oumar Barry, Mamadou Mbodji, Yolande Govindama, Breeda Mc Grath, Floretta Boonzaier, Shose Kessi, and Lewis Gordon.

To Hussein Bulhan and Chalmer Thompson. Thank you again for your trust. I am forever grateful for this opportunity. I am so grateful for your mentorship and generosity, and I really hope that my work will be at the level of your expectations.

Every piece of your advice and word of support gives me strength to keep on working.

To
Malik,
Kamil and
Nayla Barry

my children who do not cease to challenge me. You make me grow. I am so honored to be part of your journey into this world.

And to my grandmother Mrs Diop, Sira Sissoko Sakiliba, a true feminist who inspired generations to build a brighter future and claim the life they deserved.

Contents

1

Introduction

This new publication introduces the topic of adornment and masquerade in African femininity. This title evokes womanliness and its levels of representation in society individually and generally. Adornment is defined as something decorative or the art of decorating something or someone. For women, it refers to clothes, accessories, hairstyle, or even make-up used to enhance their attractiveness. Adornment is a wide department comprising a universe of possible body treatments and techniques. Each culture has its own strategies and artistry in this field. Indeed, anthropologists have noted that the body can adorn itself with or without accessories, with the example of tattoos and scarifications. The gait and other body techniques, like dancing, also are representative of femininity.

In our previous publication in this collection, we have analyzed feminine figures in African oral tradition, and provided explanations on their construction. We have shown the ambivalence of these characters, and its illustration in literature. Femininity and maternity are also representations of this ambivalence. Indeed, they suggest different dispositions and status in women's lives. This ambivalence is rooted in the premises of our consciousness through our primary relationship to the first Other and our construction of narcissism and alterity. This primary relationship has

I. S. Diop, *Adornment, Masquerade and African Femininity*, Pan-African Psychologies,
https://doi.org/10.1007/978-3-031-28748-0_1

reflected on the representation of the world, this binary conception of the beginnings as the base of our system of thinking. Indeed, this ambivalent image of the mother has stayed in the collective unconscious and evolved to the mirrored figures of the saint mother and the provocative sexually attractive woman. Therefore, another representation has emerged: that of unpredictable and insatiable nature opposed to the organized and ruled representation of religion. We can observe this opposition in tales where the devouring mother is facing the hero, for her defeat to be the founding act of civilization and order.

Femininity refers to women's attractiveness, and seduction. It calls to men's erotic representation of women, their image as objects of desire. Whereas maternity refers to sacrifice and women's purity, connected to the image of the sacred woman detached from sexuality and committed to motherhood.

In our previous research on the topic of hysterectomy and mastectomy, we recognized these concepts in women's speeches, and were able to analyze them related to breasts and uterus as symbolic organs. Since this question was always at the center of our research, we have investigated years ago the topic of the cross-cultural approach to postpartum depression, to understand how this gap between motherhood and femininity is viewed in different cultures, especially in Africa. We chose the context of postpartum because it is a moment when the woman ceases to be the carrier of her baby, and they both become members of the community. This moment of separation is important because of its narcissistic implications. This is when the founding moment of the psychic construction is replayed in reverse mode, and the woman has the chance to become her own Maternal Other and gain omnipotence in her turn. Restituting her baby to the community and renouncing her savage maternal instincts is a symbolic castration that is specific to the woman who becomes a mother. When it comes to femininity, it catches the eye, ear, and smell of the viewer, to lure them into believing that they are needed, for the woman to be complete, and achieve this omnipotence. However, the goal is for the woman never to attain this frightening state of omnipotence, as it echoes the viewer's own archaic anguish. Hence, it gives birth to the game of masquerade and parade.

Authors in psychoanalysis have theorized the question of womanhood as an interrogation never to be responded to, because of its mystery. This question mark is the sign that best represents the woman, since she embodies the very concept of desire. The lack she represents is at the source of her quest: "she desires to be desired" until she desires beyond the Other's gaze. There she attains her own jouissance. Feminine masquerade appears not only as an individual psychoanalytic representation, but also a social construct, as it is supported by cultural traditions.

Our goal as a psychologist was to grasp the duality of women and understand their position as destination and source of desire. We wanted to use this knowledge of psychoanalysis to understand what these interventions meant for them as women and as humans. Being an African woman put us in a position to approach this question, with the perspective to give voice to other African women and understand how this ambivalence takes place in their lived experience and our own. Our research associated to our clinical practice has brought us to develop a psychosocial tool using some specific tales, showing the devouring mother, and we have observed patients' reactions to this character. This unique reading of sociocultural signs allows us to find levers of improvement for clinical practice. We have chosen to actively participate in the development of this discipline in Africa because we believe that African cultural concepts must be used to resolve issues and promote transmission in society.

The problematic of this book is how adornment can be the space of the expression for this ambivalence and mark the body as a desiring subject. We will also try to understand how it plays the masquerade of femininity and contributes to self-expression either as a coping strategy or a vehicle of emancipation in society. To serve this purpose we will use the concepts of Maternal Other and Great Other, as proposed in the Lacanian theory. The Maternal Other is the first encounter with alterity, through the mother–child primary relationship, siege of the ambivalence previously explained in this introduction. The Great Other is the representation of Law, as a third part in the fusional primary relationship, witness to all exchanges, and relayed by the paternal figure, also representing the Lacanian concept of the Name-of-the-Father.

In the second chapter, we will focus on the body to understand how early interactions and body treatments contribute to shaping the mind, determining the woman in her social role and initiating her in the use of adornment as the art of mastering the other's gaze. We will present the concept of Ego-Skin and discuss how these interactions have an impact on narcissism and self-representation. This will allow us to discuss alterity and mother–child separation in the Senegalese context, through the work of authors who have analyzed the moment of weaning as fundamental to the inclusion of others in the fusional relationship.

In the third chapter, we will focus on the ambivalence in women's representation. we will discuss how the ambivalence between divinity and sorcery is a conversion of the same ambivalence between maternity and femininity. We will take as examples representations of feminine mythological and religious figures and analyze how beauty is represented as a symbol of purity or as a weapon.

In the fourth chapter, I demonstrate how adornment with clothes and accessories represents the difference between social classes. I will describe how in the history of some African ethnic groups, social classes and totemic groups could be recognized through their clothes, jewels, hairstyles, and fabrics. We will show how this history remains in the collective unconscious. We will also analyze the purpose and nature of ritual clothes and accessories, to understand their symbolic meaning.

In the fifth chapter, we will observe how adornment and references of female beauty have evolved through the years because of colonialism. We will see how it can be used as a form of expression, assimilation, or marginalization. With our perspective as a clinical psychology, we will see how it connects to our psychological construction and links with the concept of Ego-Skin, as Belliard discusses in her work. Finally, we will interrogate pro-African and pro-natural hair movements on the continent and think about their motivation and goal for the reconstruction of a decolonized representation of self. In fact, we will see how decolonial feminism has an important role in the acceptance of African women at all levels for themselves, for their community, and for the world.

In the sixth chapter, we will return to the dual representation of women as the Great Other and Maternal Other. We will discuss structural concepts of Jacques Lacan, in perspective with the theoretical views of Lemoine-Luccioni on feminine masquerade. We will rebound on our previous publication about African mythology to bring a new perspective to these approaches. Then, we will go through the literature in psychoanalysis and psychotherapy to observe the conception of feminine masquerade and how it is represented in some African societies. There, we will make connections with the work of Eugénie Lemoine-Luccioni and Jacques Lacan about femininity and masquerade. Here we will analyze the symbolic aspects of adornment and self-representation as a mirroring identification to female powerful figures. We will question the relationship between men and women, in the game of power and social roles. This section will be the occasion to explain the challenges of the actual society: to recognize women in their rightful position, and for women to detach themselves from socially assigned representations.

In the seventh chapter, we will analyze some clinical examples of psychotherapy patients to demonstrate the symbolism of adornment and how it reflects power and illusion. We will present the stories of two women who have undergone psychological transformation after critical surgical interventions. We will see how they operated this reconstruction and what it revealed of adornment and masquerade. Mrs A.'s and Mrs M.'s testimonies will be analyzed to show how their lived experience is instructive of women's approach to emancipation. The discussion and theoretical-clinical analysis will help us understand how they illustrate coping strategies and structuring narcissism.

The last chapter will be the conclusion, aiming to finally respond to our problematic. From our perspective as a clinical psychologist and researcher, we will discuss further questions, and potential developments.

2

Representation of the Feminine Body

2.1 Sculpting a Body

2.1.1 The Body in the Social Dynamic

Mauss (1950a) theorized the concept of body techniques in his work. He defined these as "how men in each society have a traditional manner of using their bodies." We will introduce these techniques and their importance in the assignment of social roles. Mauss (1950b) has developed an immense work about gift and exchange. He analyzed the structure of exchanges in different cultures, identifying a pattern showing that each act of giving and receiving is an actualization of an ancient mythological figure that anthropologists called *Property Woman*. Giving earns *mana* (internal power and authority) to the giver, and he must stay in a position of balance to keep it and maintain this representation of similarity to the primary figure of authority. The system of trade and alliance remains inherent to the group and is transmitted from one generation to another, preserving a relationship to this maternal figure. In other words, Mauss's representation of culture is this repetition of cycles through exchanges

I. S. Diop, *Adornment, Masquerade and African Femininity*, Pan-African Psychologies,
https://doi.org/10.1007/978-3-031-28748-0_2

actualizing the primary relationship with this maternal superego owner of everything. We cannot help but draw a link to the Kleinian representation of the maternal superego full of everything the baby is envious of (milk, tenderness, power, feces). Indeed, in the Kleinian representation of the maternal primary figure in the first four months of life, the archaic maternal superego gathers all negative feelings and experiences and exposes the baby to the image of an all-powerful mother whose body collects and keeps everything the child wants, initiating the feeling of envy, central in Klein's theory. In brief, the primary act of life is giving, and the first human giver is the mother.

Body techniques are tools people use to pass along culture from the youngest age. There are specific ways of carrying, nursing, and taking care of a child, depending on their gender, position, and social situation. We can imagine how rituals play a specific role in these mothering techniques and analyze them as references to the abstraction, dictating the order of generation. This authority granting what Mauss calls *mana* prevents humans from breaking fundamental rules defining the courses of the exchange between people: the prohibition of incest and the obligation of exogamy. When giving away their siblings and children for marriage, men and women earn and keep *mana* and perpetuate the exchange cycle, renouncing their feelings of envy and jealousy.

Many anthropologists have been interested in understanding the symbolism of rites of passage. Mauss has described how adolescence is critical in teaching these techniques and, more specifically, how the relationship between genders is defined and codified at this age and during these rites. Thus, we can imagine how they play an essential role in teaching girls how to become women and use their bodies as a tool in society to take an active position in this exchange cycle.

Jacqueline Rabain's book *L'enfant du lignage* (1979) is a rich piece where the author observes children with their families in Wolof and Sereer households. She analyzes the role of social interactions in children's education. According to her, they go through different steps when learning to be a part of their communities. The first step is when they are still being breastfed. At this moment, "the feeding turns into a game[1] of hiding and seek, watching and being watched, touching and being touched" (1979: 41). Children explore the limitations of their mother's body and the space around them. "They take a position in the social territory, passing from one adult or elder to the other, testing their limits" (1979: 41). The community significantly participates in breastfeeding through verbal expressions, implying that this space created by breastfeeding does not solely belong to mother and child but is also under the legislation of the ancestors and the society. Therefore, this primary exploration of the other's body leads the child to consider a more expansive frame: the law of society that commands the rules of exchange. To this point, the child knows their affiliation to a lineage and becomes a community member and a relative. Rabain insists on the participation of family members, elders, and peers in this process, alleviating the parental pressure, and underlying their roles. The weaning phase marks the father's introduction as the new primary giver. The father offers sweets and presents as a motivation for the child to renounce breastfeeding, drawing a new opportunity for separation and exchange, thus standing as the new giver. The process of mediation reduces frustration in different settings. Rabain shows some interactions where the child expresses her anger through this weaning phase. She describes how the community hosts the child and intervenes. The elders play an essential role in this situation because they integrate their sibling into their group, showing them the advantages of growing up, and introducing them to games and conversations. Some of the body techniques described by Mauss are introduced by peers, as they learn to take care of each other and remember to be elders and future parents. The author underlines the importance of this horizontal perspective in understanding the family constellation to grasp the complexity of transmission instead of focusing on the role of the parental dyad as sole educators. The learning experience emphasizes the group's representation as a space of interaction and exchange through the body and kinesthetic

[1] Translated and explained from original quote in French: "L'allaitement est prétexte et se transforme en jeu de corps à corps, en jeu de cache-cache orchestré, comme ici, par la mère (être dissimulé / être regardé, être proche / être à distance). Les retours à la mère s'intercalent et donnent leur rythme à un parcours exploratoire, à une prise de possession d'un territoire social."

exploration during the first years. Children integrate their rightful place in the exchange cycle among their peers and learn their position with regard to parents and elders.

As Jacqueline Rabain describes this primary education phase, we identify the essential dimension of the body in every interaction as the principal surface of exchange. Moreover, the body remains the first indication of diagnosis and vehicle of treatment in traditional therapies. Ritual and mothering techniques also target the body, such as massages and holding. Although massages have the advantage of enhancing babies' motricity and early physical development, they are different depending on gender. According to beauty standards, girls' massages emphasize breasts, hips, and buttocks, whereas boys' massages enhance their agility and muscles and widen their shoulders. This configuration shows how body treatment since early childhood and social roles are significantly linked. Rabain discusses how Islam has brought a new body representation as "it must be mortified, purified of its stain, stripped of its sensory and motor thickness by appropriate disciplines."[2] However, she notices that children's religious education does not start before age six, until then, rules of social distanciation and body decency do not apply.

Discussing Rabain's theories in relation to Mauss's, we can summarize our point along the following lines. Firstly, each culture has a specific mythology defining its architecture and functioning: an exchange mechanism at the center of each functioning that organizes relationships between community members. The community identifies social roles and teaches individuals how to fit in their position early on. This teaching is a part of traditional education, through mechanisms like body techniques, introduced by parents and relayed by elders and peers. Secondly, this body investment from the earliest age imprints sensoriality and kinesthetic representation, making the physical experience significant to one's psychological representations of oneself. Lastly, this verbal and

[2] Translated from original quote in French P.81: "L'Islam introduit un changement dans la représentation du corps. Celui-ci doit être mortifié, purifié de sa souillure, dépouillé de son épaisseur sensorielle et motrice par des disciplines appropriées."

physical interaction frame shapes one's representation of the Other as a peer or a legislator, subsequently confronting them with castration. Therefore, these authors have shown through their theories that the body is at the center of social representation in West African traditional education. Body techniques underline individual positions and shape boundaries between individuals.

Moreover, in addition to social and educational interactions, body techniques point to the rules and correct community members' mistakes. Community participative education through hand touching and holding is essential for communication since it pacifies human conflicts. In contrast, simple observation and compliments arouse mistrust, possibly hiding envy and jealousy, synonyms for misfortune. We can see how physical interactions are fundamental for general communication and social cohesion.

Claude Lévi-Strauss has contributed a significant work on women in society's exchange cycle. He was interested in the rules of language, and particularly in the words prohibited in various cultures. According to him, "all these prohibitions thus come down to a common denominator: they constitute an abuse of language, and they are, as such, grouped with the prohibition of incest, or with acts evocative of incest. What does this mean, if not that women are treated as abused signs when they are not given the use reserved. Their purpose is to be communicated. Thus, the language and the exogamy would represent two solutions to the same fundamental situation. Unfortunately, the first one has reached a high degree of perfection; the second has remained approximate and precarious. But this inequality is not without counterpart"[3] (Lévi-Strauss (1967) *Les structures élémentaires de la parenté*, p. 568). This metaphor expresses the symbolism of language as representative of society, as a system created by rules, and alterity. It exists because of the mere introduction of alterity.

[3] Translated from original quote in French: "toutes ces prohibitions se ramènent donc à un dénominateur commun: elles constituent un abus de langage, et elles sont, à ce titre, groupées avec la prohibition de l'inceste, ou avec des actes évocateurs de l'inceste. Qu'est-ce que cela signifie, sinon que les femmes, elles-mêmes, sont traitées comme des signes dont on abuse, quand on ne leur donne pas l'emploi réservés aux signes, c'est-à-dire d'être communiqués. Ainsi le langage et l'exogamie représenteraient deux solutions à une même situation fondamentale. La première a atteint un haut degré de perfection; la seconde est restée approximative et précaire. Mais cette inégalité n'est pas sans contrepartie" (Les structures élémentaires de la parenté, p. 568).

In this configuration, as much as women and men are members of society, they are identified in this metaphor as signs of language. Therefore, as much as rules apply in society about how relationships with women are organized (marriage, rites, etc.), language also has rules.

According to Lévi-Strauss, the woman is a sign transmitted to represent the alliance between groups, families, and generations. She is a joint that binds men together and allows them to find common ground to ensure their societies' evolution. Thus, a woman is similar to language and has the exact property to communicate and share for an alliance. Indeed, both are present, at the same time, in all societies. Thus, the role of culture is to set up these two types of language and prevent any forbidden use of these signs.

However, this is not so simple because "in men's matrimonial dialogue, the woman is never purely, a topic because, if in general, they represent a certain category of signs, intended for a certain type of communication, each woman, preserves a particular value, which comes from her talent, before and after the marriage, to hold her part in a duet. Thus, contrary to the mere word, become an integral sign, the woman has become a value. Therefore, gender relations have preserved this affective richness, this fervor, and this mystery, which have undoubtedly imprinted, at the origin, the whole universe of human communications."[4]

In short, men and women are signs that have different values, and culture is a set of rules for combining them. These rules evolve with new combinations of languages that the signs produce, as they are both products and producers of culture. Language is based on roles and giving because it draws links between individuals and is a product of culture. Understanding how one finds their place in society requires one to read the codes and techniques of social roles.

[4]Translated from original quote in French: "Dans le dialogue matrimonial des hommes, la femme n'est jamais purement, ce dont on parle, car si les hommes, en général, représentent une certaine catégorie de signes, destinés à un certain type de communication, chaque femme, conserve une valeur particulière, qui provient de son talent, avant et après le mariage, à tenir sa partie dans un duo. A l'inverse du mot, devenu intégralement signe, la femme est donc restée, en même temps que signe, valeur. Ainsi s'explique que les relations entre les sexes aient préservé cette richesse affective, cette ferveur et ce mystère, qui ont sans doute imprégné, à l'origine tout l'univers des communications humaines" (Les structures élémentaires de la parenté, p. 569).

The following section will discuss how Western psychologists have understood the impact of mothering techniques and early interactions on psychological structuration.

2.1.2 Mothering and Early Psychological Construction

Hélène Stork (1986) has concentrated her research on primary interaction and mothering techniques and their meaning in cultural representations. She underlined Rabain's work about the essential phase of breastfeeding and weaning as representative of the culturally mediated double maternal function: nurturing and handling. The social mediation process is crucial to maintain an opening for the weaning child to gain his autonomy and social position. In addition, society plays a key role when introducing the father as the new giver, representing his capacity to support his family (money, candies, activities).

Stork has underlined how this connection between mother and child is a priority and is a critical factor for safe development. For example, she refers to the term proximal interaction to describe how the mother's body adjusts to her child's. Mothering techniques, like massages, aim to draw the skin borders and enhance the baby's body representation.

Didier Anzieu has originated the Ego-Skin concept. He describes it as: "a figuration that the child's Ego uses during the early phases of development to represent itself as the Ego psychic contents, integrated from its experience at the body's surface. When the psychic Ego distinguishes from the bodily Ego on the operational level and remains confused with it on the figurative level."[5] This concept is close to the phase mentioned by Rabain and Stork, who discuss the proximal interaction between mother and child and its effect on the latter's representation of himself and the Other. When mothering techniques and bodily experiences build this Ego-Skin, they mark a difference between an inside and an outside.

---

[5] Translated from original quote in French: "Par Moi-peau, je désigne une figuration dont le Moi de l'enfant se sert au cours des phases précoces de son développement pour se représenter lui-même comme Moi contenant les contenus psychiques, à partir de son expérience de la surface du corps. Cela correspond au moment où le Moi psychique se différencie du Moi corporel sur le plan opératif et reste confondu avec lui sur le plan figurative."

The Ego-Skin as a concept helps to understand how primary interactions contribute to building body image and representation. In the previous paragraphs, we discussed how early years and weaning are the moments when the child learns his place and role in society. The act of giving determines each one's place in the hierarchy. Referring to Anzieu's (1995) work at this stage of our reasoning is essential to apprehend the reminiscence of this Ego-Skin on the actual bodily experience throughout life. We hypothesize that adornment is closely linked to this concept and underlines the narcissistic aspects of our personality.

Moreover, primary models of interactions and integration of social roles have imprinted standards and representations that influence one's perception of self.

In the next section, we will discuss the representation of women in myths and tales. Finally, we will see how this can actualize and judge certain qualities or faults in girls' education.

2.2 A Beautiful Mind

2.2.1 Influential Feminine Figures in African Mythology

In the previous section, we focused on primary interactions shaping the Ego-Skin. We will now examine the beliefs behind body treatments, body techniques, and education. On the one hand, the bodily experience of maternal handling shapes this primary Ego, staying at the surface of one's identity. On the other hand, these handling experiences convey images of womanhood and its social ideal. In addition, there exists a network of representations, supporting images of womanhood that are socially valued and others that are not. I have identified some figures that represent this paradox by analyzing African mythology and tales.

I have previously published the book Diop (2019). In this writing, I aimed to introduce feminine figures of African mythology and their impact on the representations of womanhood, motherhood, and femininity. This section will describe how these representations have a crucial role in girls' education. More specifically, I will discuss the role of adornment and aesthetics in describing these feminine figures of African mythology.

Influential feminine figures in African mythology often appear dangerous. Mami Wata is an exciting example of how women's seduction can be deadly. In most countries, she has a connection with water and is often associated with mermaids, hence the root "water" in her name. She comes out at night, usually in downtown areas. Mami Wata seduces men and offers a contract; she grants them money and power for their exclusive love and sexuality. Their disobedience may cost them their mind and wealth. This description of femininity associated with seduction, lust, and dangerousness can explain social representations of women's emancipation. Women sex workers are associated with Mami Wata in many countries because they are out at night and represent seduction and debauchery. In this previous research, I studied how the qualification for both sex workers and divorced women is "free women." This qualification transcribes society's fear of exercising sexuality out of a marriage setting.

However, the increasing number of divorces globally tends to change this representation, even though in Senegal the wish of many divorced women is still to eventually remarry. In the standard narrative, a happy woman is a married woman, stable in a permanent relationship. This idea is an image and a life goal that women in African societies are more likely to have as personal ambition.

The representation of Mami Wata as an overtly sexually appealing woman is an extreme image of women stepping away from the rules but still the object of men's desire. Therefore, they induce a glimpse of tricks and ideas that engaged women can use to entertain and keep their men from these seductive women. In this configuration, men are infantilized as seduced and fooled by the most skillful woman. Moreover, they are not responsible for their actions since it is their nature to fall for seductive women. Women are supposed to navigate between their social role as wives and mothers and their position as objects of men's desires. This schematic view of their lives does not leave much space for individual and professional accomplishment.

Furthermore, a professional accomplishment for a woman can never be complete when acquired without an ordinary family life. Such success will be considered as obtained at the expense of a family. Emancipation comes with the sacrifice of marriage since society is not ready to accept women in positions of power. This rejection marginalizes emancipated women, and hence this connection with figures like Mami Wata and sex workers. Women in positions of power, financially supporting their families, often face the stigma of unfit women. Their relatives will ask for financial support but never acknowledge their success, leaving them feeling used and judged.

2.2.2 Good Women and Suitable Mothers

Against these influential figures of deadly seductive women, societies have built the concept of the good woman and benevolent mother, appearing in tales as the hero's mother. This character is redundant in African tales, always facing rivalry and wickedness with pride and discrete strength. This attitude of bearing suffering without complaint is highly valued, especially in West Africa and, more specifically, in marital relationships with husband and in-laws.

Boubacar Ly (1966) underlines the Senegalese concept *Ndeye-Ju-liggey*, meaning the mother who has worked well. Their children's success and accomplishment will be the compensation for their effort and sacrifice. In most tales, the hero is born into a world dominated by a mighty witch in a matriarchal society. His mother is a benevolent woman, often modest or poor; she raises him to become their people's savior through sacrifice and suffering. When the hero defeats the witch, he puts the power back into men's hands, and his mother finally attains the position she deserves.

In some cases, the benevolent mother's endeavor justifies promoting the cultural values of women's submission to their husbands or potential husbands. However, although the ordinary family as the safest environment for children remains a common standard encouraged by society, most of the effort to maintain this stability rests on the wife's shoulders. Therefore, education finds its meaning in teaching girls and women how to become wives and make the right sacrifices for the greater good. The role of handling and body techniques is to promote healthy development for the child, shape his body, and strengthen his muscles. In contrast, the role of education is more about shaping the mind and making it fit, taming the unpredictable aspects of womanhood. Personality traits like patience, tenderness, generosity, and listening are promoted for girls because they define a good wife.

Conversely, stubbornness, curiosity, recklessness, envy, and irritability will not be encouraged because they would challenge a husband's choice or decision. We observe this paradox when analyzing the description of mighty feminine figures in African mythology. For example, the character of the witch Ndjeddo Dewal, analyzed in my previous publication, is curious, envious, wicked, greedy, and irritable, in opposition to the hero's mother, who is tender, calm, generous, docile, and listens to her child.

In parallel to the conflict between the hero and the witch, there is another fight: two mothering models in opposition. On the one hand, the witch is a devouring mother, ravaging the village with her seven daughters cherished and spoiled. Moreover, on the other hand, the benevolent mother is firm and teaches her son to live with little or no resources. This classic conflict between these two education models often surfaces in family rivalry when comparing children's successes. However, again, in the end, the mother is judged through her children's evaluation. An important descriptive aspect of the benevolent mother is that she never intervenes to save the hero and stands back resigned to accept his fate.

Society judges women's education model, nature, qualities, faults, and relationships with their husband, in-laws, and co-wives. Mothers' role as primary carers for their daughters is to teach them the management of their emotions into socially acceptable behaviors. They prepare them to face the hardships of women's lives and make the same sacrifices they made in their time.

In women's narratives, we observe how they receive little help from their mothers in facing the challenges of marriage, echoing the role of the benevolent mother as silent observers. Usually, they encourage their daughters to face suffering as one of life's challenges and be faithful for a better end to compensate for their effort. Their father's or uncle's intervention in couple mediation has a good impact because it often legitimates their complaints and makes their voices heard, as adults and peers to their husbands. However, the main reason for their mother not to intervene is the fear of breaking up their daughter's marriage and being responsible for their failure. Therefore, mothers put their feelings aside to promote society's ideal of being married and stable as the best possible outcome for a woman's life.

Adornment enhances feminine advantages but is also a code sending a specific message about a woman's nature. Girls are more likely to develop a taste for their aesthetic, hair and skin treatment, and clothes during education because society reinforces this interest. Taking care of their aesthetic is part of their education and becomes a determining aspect of their personality as adults. One crucial advantage for a woman to please a husband is her beauty and capacity to convey a good image. Adornment is a set of tools that she can use to express her talent and fitness regarding her husband's desire and her superiority compared to other women.

2.2.3 Women's Emancipation and Social Representation

Feminine figures of African mythology are often wealthy, sometimes beautiful, and wear rich clothes and jewelry. In other cases, they have the power to change shape and personify men's desires. Their main power is using their image to control men's feelings and fool them. Moreover, female emancipation is usually connected to financial freedom, allowing women to care for themselves. In this aspect, they can arouse suspicion about the origin of their money. Some independent women[6] have reported being suspected by their families of being sex workers because they could not imagine them obtaining that money in any other way.

Furthermore, since they are "just" women, social stigma represents them as unable to earn such an amount in a legal working environment. This connection between emancipation and sexuality resurfaces, in this analogy, underlining the distaste of society for independent women. In this context, an adornment is a tool for these women to dress richly to show their economic power or dress soberly to disguise their strength. On the one hand, showing their wealth through adornment grants access to

[6] From my own clinical practice.

social recognition in higher classes of society. On the other hand, they can use it like armor against stereotypes and prejudices. Then it can also be seen as a personal interest and a way to express themselves through clothing and accessories to reveal their tastes.

When women hide their wealth by dressing soberly, the explanation usually relates to the fear of envy and bad luck. Society threatens their integrity, and they must hide and disguise themselves to avoid solicitations. In the country where they are known and recognized, they will not show their wealth. Only if they travel abroad will they feel free to express themselves. Being outside of their countries releases them from their chains and allows them to occupy the powerful position they have earned but cannot enjoy at home.

Furthermore, expatriation is an alternative to remove oneself from social standards that do not represent one's ambition. Society can be very intrusive and destructive to its members who will not comply with the rules. When they find themselves in this position, women can choose this alternative and subtract themselves from social standards. It is easier to be considered a stranger abroad than an alien within their own families in this context. Codes of women's conduct include their social positions, manners, speech, dress code, and attitude. This code consists of a complex system of representation conveyed in education. Being different and ambitious to attain another status can be seen as audacious and threatening for social balance. However, female independence will be accepted if families take advantage of it and cover it under a marital setting.

When society marginalizes emancipated women, it operates the exact mechanism used for mighty feminine figures to avoid disseminating a bad example and repetition in the younger generation. Thus, it is clear that emancipated women threaten the permanence of social order rules. The ferocity of Mami Wata and Ndjeddo Dewal confirms this as they are vital threats for men and their families.

The benevolent mother is usually sober and sometimes poor, incarnating suffering and abnegation. Nevertheless, her acceptance of fate and faith in a better ending gives her a purpose. In tales, this character never fights back but silently focuses on her children, despite others' wickedness and aggression. She is rewarded with her child's success, the hero who forces everyone to recognize her value. This representation confirms the realization of *Ndeyju Ligguey* because it explains the suffering and hope for a better ending. In this context, the suffering is an effort to invest in children's success, as if mothers were the sole parents involved in their development. However, this representation also legitimates rivalry and wickedness in society. People play the role of obstacle on the benevolent mother's path, only for the rise of children to supposedly provide balance and justice in the future.

Exploring the reference to adornment for the character of the benevolent mother in African mythology and tales shows us how society draws a link between poverty or soberness and purity. This character appears to be realistic when her physical appearance represents her suffering. She does not look demanding or greedy and is content with the little she has. As a reference to this representation of perfection, there are standards of adornment in society that represent an ideal for women's appearance. They are taught through education, drawing a clear link between women's image in society and their aesthetic standards, clothes, and hairstyles. We can also find this analogy in European tales, where the poor character is the victim of the wealthier and finally finds unexpected love. She is usually depicted as simple and satisfied with what she has, compared to the other character who is more prosperous and powerful and is described as insatiable.

Therefore, we can refer to dress codes determining styles that are appreciated socially and others that are not because of their association with a specific feminine image. Even though women can choose their appearance, society still judges their hairstyle, skin treatment, dress code, and even nail style. Despite the augmentation of accessories available for them, their male counterparts do not equally attract this attention.

Meanwhile, forms of expression through body treatments are increasing (tattoos, piercing, skin bleaching, surgical transformations) and are becoming available for all at a lower price. Despite judgment and interferences of cultural and religious leaders about women's appearances, women's adornment evolves, and they thrive on finding alternatives.

Society leads women to play a specific role because of this cultural background charged with social representations of women's status, appearance, and personality. Our question is how primary bodily experiences shape women's representation of their bodies and how they appear in the exchange cycle and communicate through body language and aesthetics. The following section will introduce the theories of body image and corporal scheme as they shape the entire bodily experience. We will use the example of hysterectomy and mastectomy as they change the mapping of women's bodies, to understand the symbolic value of breasts and uterus in women's status.

2.3 Shape and Boundaries

Twelve years ago, I conducted my doctoral research on hysterectomy, mastectomy, and their effects on Senegalese women's status. Consequently, I was interested in body image, its construction, and its importance for self-representation. In this section, I will introduce the work of Schilder and Dolto on body image. Then I will analyze the effect of breasts and uterus on body image and representations of motherhood and femininity. Secondly, I will discuss how their loss can impact body image and femininity, and finally, how adornment can be used strategically for compensation or narcissistic reconstruction.

Paul Schilder (1950) speaks of the postural model of the body (p. 35). This concept designates the awareness, explicit or implicit, at each moment of the individual situation of the different parts of the body. It relates to location, position, or movement. The practice of sport trains and refines this plane of our body in our mind. Schilder works on body image and introduces the notion of the libidinal structure (p. 139).

The body image includes the body schema and the representation of our whole body in our mind (p. 35). It is a conscious representation that one can have of oneself. This image carries social representations and is built only by confrontation with the social standard-type or model of desirability (tall, thin, long legs, according to the Euro-American criteria, or curves, firmness of the body, elegance, according to the African criteria). Its subjectivity is also considerable, and psychological work can contribute to rectifying it and installing it in the acceptance of oneself and not only in conformity to the ideal model. Much research and various experiments (as indicated by Schilder (1950)) have shown that everything particular in the libidinal structures reflects in the structure of the body postural model. For example, individuals with dominant impulses would feel that a certain point is an erogenous zone corresponding to this specific impulse, gathering its energy in the center of their body image.

2.3.1 Body Image and Postural Scheme

According to Schilder, it is with the hands that we discover a large part of our body. The hands themselves are an external world for the parts of the body they touch. The different parts of the body have more or fewer possibilities to feed and move to each other, and this fact is of most importance from the psychological point of view: the parts of the body that the hand can reach easily differ in their psychological structure from those that it can reach only with difficulty. The eyes also play an essential role in elaborating body image, and the parts of the body that are visible are supposedly different from those that are not. The sole individual's activity is not enough to build the body image; others' intervention, touching, and interest in various body parts also have enormous importance in postural development. As soon as, one way or another, one of the body image elements gains importance, it affects the body's internal balance.

Schilder also observes the modifications caused by the pain of body image, mainly through hypochondria (p. 164). According to him, organic pain leads to immediate changes in the libidinal structure of the body image. Narcissistic libido invades the painful part and overloads the body's postural model. The painful organ becomes the center of the body's new learning experience and takes over the role of the erogenous zones. Finally, Schilder evokes modifications of body image in hysteria by indicating that when the changes affecting body image symbolize the sexual organ, it is closely associated with the current sexual relations with others, considered globally (p. 186).

From Schilder's work, we can draw the following points:

- The postural model and body image are entities in constant evolution through our experiences and the influence of our environment.
- Organs of the body have variable importance depending on their function and the attention they attract from us and others.

Dolto (1984) distinguishes body image and body schema, and emphasizes the first concept. According to this author, the "body schema is a reality of fact; it is our physical lived experience, in contact with the world. Experiences of our reality depend on the organism's integrity, its transitory or permanent lesions, neurological, muscular, osseous, and our visceral, circulatory physiological sensations - they are still called coenesthetic" (p. 18). Thus, the body schema comes from our reality and experiences; early organic attacks can impact it due to the insufficiency or interruption of language relations. These early organic attacks can cause disorders of the body schema, leading to temporary or durable modifications of body image.

Dolto defines body image for a human being, as the element that is permanently "the unconscious remanent representation where his desire is born" (p. 34). It is not the same type of anatomical data as the body schema can be. Instead, it is always a potential phantasmatic image of communication, collecting the relational experiences of need and desire, valorizing or devaluing, "narcissizing or de-narcissizing" (p. 37). These valorizing or devaluing sensations symbolize variations of perception in the body schema and, more particularly, those induced by interhuman encounters. Mothering techniques play a crucial role in this symbolization process because they draw the borders of each body, marking an inside and an outside.

Dolto distinguishes three modalities in the body image: the basic, the functional, and the erogenous image, "which constitute and ensure the image of the living body and the subject's narcissism at each stage of its evolution"[7] (p. 49).

The basic image is what allows the child to feel himself in some kind of consistency, a narcissistic or a space–time continuity that remains and is fleshed out from his birth, despite his life's mutations, the displacements imposed on his body, and the struggles he has to go through (p. 50).

Whereas the basic image has a static dimension, the functional image is a subject's sthenic image, aiming to achieve his desire. The functional

---

[7]Translated from original quote in French: "lesquelles toutes ensemble constituent et assurent l'image du corps vivant et le narcissisme du sujet à chaque stade de son évolution" (p. 49).

image is driven by life impulses and, after being subjectivized in desire, leads the subject toward pleasure, objectifying him to the world and others.

Finally, the erogenous image is the place that concentrates pleasure or erotic displeasure with the other. Its representation refers "to circles, ovals, concaves, balls, palps, lines and holes, imagined endowed with active emissive or passive receptive intentions, with pleasant or unpleasant purpose"[8] (p. 57).

According to Dolto, these images are connected, permanently cohesive with the dynamic image. The latter corresponds to the "desire to be and persevere in a becoming" (p. 58). Thus, the dynamic image does not have a representation of its own.

The losses the subject will endure are "castrations" and qualified as "symbolizing." Dolto classifies the umbilical castration as the first of this list because it "originates the body schema within the limits of the skin envelope, cut off from the placenta and the envelopes included in the uterus left to it"[9] (p. 90–91). This notion of symbolic castration refers to the effect that excision or circumcision can have on body image. When realizing this research about the consequences of hysterectomy and mastectomy for Senegalese women, I hypothesized that the loss of the uterus and breast would be different for women than early genital cutting. They occur during adulthood, well after the construction of body image. Nevertheless, we will see in the last chapter that a psychic reorganization has to occur while redefining the body's limits after these operations.

Based on Schilder, Dolto, and the work of various other authors (Anzieu (2005), Blin, Parat, Gros, etc.), we have tried to explain the importance of the breast and the uterus in the body schema and the body image, and the representations attached to them. We will also call upon the concepts of motherhood and femininity to demonstrate their symbolism.

---

[8] Translated from original quote in French: "à des cercles, ovales, concaves, boules, palpes, traits et trous, imaginés doués d'intentions émissives actives ou réceptives passives, à but agréables ou désagréables" (p. 57).

[9] Translated from original quote in French: "origine le schéma corporel dans les limites de l'enveloppe, qui est la peau, coupée du placenta et des enveloppes incluses dans l'utérus, et à lui laissées" (p. 90–91).

2.3.2 Symbolic Organs of Femininity and Maternity

Breasts play an essential role in femininity and a woman's body image. The biological function of breasts is to produce milk to nurse a newborn. The physiological importance of milk and the psychological importance of breasts arouse all sorts of representations.

When associated with milk, breasts take a magic-religious value in some cultures. For example, in Turkish folklore, one imagines a "lake of milk" and a supernatural nourishing mother (Roux, 1967, p. 51). Sometimes, in Central Asian shamanism, the lake is represented as a female individual, named "Mother-Lake-of-Milk,"[10] a goddess, avatar of the nurturing mother of the first man, coming out of the cosmic cave naked to the waist (Roux, 1967, p. 52). We cannot help but recall here Mauss's findings about the *Property Woman*, primary giver, as life and milk can be considered as the first gifts.

Freud evoked a dissociated representation of breasts in his works: "A woman's breast evokes at the same time hunger and love"[11] (1967, p. 181). Hélène Parat insists on this dissociation. According to this author, breast-milk incarnating motherhood stays separated from femininity because of the prohibition of incest. It could lead to a dangerous confusion between mother and woman, appealing to the unconscious permanence of Oedipal wishes (2007, p. 9).

According to Anne Anzieu, a woman is born incomplete, and her body takes shape throughout her life. Breasts confirm this idea of incompleteness because their shape changes continuously, modifying the body. This author relies on the idea of Didier Anzieu, according to whom the transformations of the female body will influence the topography of the determined psychic space. Because of their late appearance and role, breasts have crucial importance in body image.

Dominique Blin (2007, p. 120) addresses the topics of breastfeeding, a woman's body, and the value of breastmilk. According to this author, the physical transformation of the body in breastfeeding reveals another

[10] Translated from original quote in French: "Mère-Lac-de-Lait," Roux (1967, p. 52).

[11] Translated from original quote in French: "Le sein de la femme évoque à la fois la faim et l'amour," Freud (1967, p. 181).

part of femininity after the body transformation undergone through pregnancy. The milk marks a woman's quality and competence as a mother; it declares the power to produce and allows her to enjoy this capacity. Blin grants to milk the property of binding together mother's and child's bodies. This property is somewhat paradoxical because as much as the milk binds together mother and child, denying a separation, it draws a limit between their bodies, a hyphen (p. 121). The author observes the representations of breastmilk and underlines a remarkable place of projection, a phantasmatic environment where impulses and instinctual and cultural images are navigated (p. 121). The interviews collected through her research reveal a comparison between breastmilk and semen. This comparison leads Blin to hypothesize a phallic enjoyment felt in the property of producing breastmilk.

Hélène Parat supported this idea. Indeed, according to her, the breastfeeding clinic allows for the visualization of the permanence and revival of partial impulses finding expression in a phantasy of liquids infiltrating maternal functioning. Furthermore, the author revisits the dissociation between erotic and nurturing breasts. She interprets this opposition as an Oedipean defensive barrier, complexifying this phantasy of liquids (milk-sperm-blood) and finding its first safeguards in the impulse endeavors of the oral, anal, and phallic breast. Finally, according to Hélène Parat (2011), these impulsive modalities of breastfeeding show that the feminine maternal breast can certainly not be univocal (p. 1612).

Hélène Deutsch (1924) underlined the sexual values of breastfeeding, describing it as "an act of sexual enjoyment during which the mammary gland plays the role of an erogenous zone. (…) As soon as the sexual role of the suckling mechanism takes too much importance, the repression intervenes" (p. 93).[12] Thus, she highlights sexual impulses at work in breastfeeding and repressive cultural prohibitions provoking this dissociation between motherhood and femininity.

Breastfeeding symbolizes generosity, dedication, and gift. Blin returned to the work of Marcel Mauss on giving. Giving guarantees a hold on the person who receives, and the gift carries paradoxical messages (p. 123). The

[12] Translated from original quote in French: "un acte de jouissance sexuelle au cours duquel la glande mammaire joue le rôle d'une zone érogène. (…) Dés que le rôle sexuel de l'appareil de succion prend trop d'importance, le refoulement intervient" (p. 93).

transmission taking place through breastfeeding seems to go beyond simple nutrition because we find in the concept of the brotherhood of milk a kinship similar to that of blood in Islam and the Wolof culture in Senegal. Delaisi de Parseval (2007) observes this phenomenon by referring to the difficulty experienced by women during weaning after the breastmilk donation, often experienced as an intense frustration (p. 55). This author also mentions that women who donate milk often also donate blood. In reviewing their testimonies, she notes the specific and temporal character of milk and a desire to transmit a family legacy inherent in the female lineage (p. 55). In the Wolof culture, breastfeeding is utterly necessary as it is viewed as giving intelligence and personality to the child (Diop, 1985: 19).

Beyond its aesthetic aspect, the breast's biological function gives it an important place, as it is the first object in the child's psychological organization. We can refer here to Schilder's work mentioned above on the libidinal structure of the body image, hypothesizing that the impulse movements carried out on breasts and their primary function increase their importance in a woman's body image.

For Gros (1983), the breast embodies the ontogeny of communication: the most archaic, universal, deepest communication, on which communication with others will probably depend. Cancer (of the breast) is one of the great disorders of communication; the sexual relationship is the most intense communication since it is a part of the communication of love. They are a primary transmission vehicle for the values a woman has received from her mother and wishes to transmit to her daughter. She learns them as specific body techniques. In the same way, this vehicle can recover the feeling of maternal omnipotence, grasped during the first moments of life. Thus, breasts represent femininity, in its phallic potency, and this is transmitted and integrated in women's social status.

Our previous research with women undergoing hysterectomy has taught us how this organ is vital to their female identity. In addition, we have studied the representation of the uterus in psychology and medicine and its evolution with women's status in society. In the history of medicine, we can see how scientists have tried to objectify and control women's bodies.

Hippocrates compared the uterus to an organ endowed with feelings and movements in ancient medicine. He supposed that this organ could be carried to various parts of the body and cause accidents. The doctor could cure his patient by calling the uterus back to its place, using fragrances to flatter its senses. In the past, theories of hysteria described it as an affection of the uterus. There was the idea of a mysterious ball, moving from the uterus through the abdomen, the thorax, the throat, going up and down, hindering the breathing, producing clenching of the throat and convulsions, and deterring intellectual faculties (Dictionary of medicine, 1824: 540). Gérard Lahouati (2000, p. 592) revisits Casanova's work about the thinking uterus and evokes the latter's representation of women's personality and sexuality as influenced by their thinking uterus. Indeed, Casanova's proposition was their submission to men, as a solution to their uterus' indiscipline.

From a religious point of view, the word "entrails" refers to the uterus, and the origin of men, denoting the "maternal entrails of God" (Ugeux, 2006:209), thus imagining a combined-gender entity as the primary giver.

In these ancient medical theories, we can see the attempt to explain the female functioning and seize control of this exclusively female organ. This organ, whose first function is supposed to be advantageous, would have, according to these theories, avatars that are at least negative. Moreover, this personification of the uterus, as a thinking being, evokes the idea of a child living inside the woman's body and traveling there at will. This idea could be a way to take away the woman's power over her body and her ability to give life. These doctors, in their reasoning, have introduced a foreign organ into the female body, over whom they have capacities of control. Then they control the uterus, whereas the woman cannot do so. In this way, one could think that they are trying to attribute to themselves the capacity of a creator, which this organ responds to and obeys. Let us establish a parallel with the theories of the Dogons of Mali on the correspondences between forms of matrices and child conception (Griaule, 1936). We find there the same idea of control and mastery of the mystery of childbirth through science.

Paul Cesbron (2008) is interested in the evolution of gynecology and obstetrics and the emergence of the male doctor, who supplanted the midwife in her role of assistance and guidance to the parturient. According to Cesbron, it is the man-doctor who, from now on, supervises the midwife, teaches her obstetrics, manages her, and organizes the care of mothers and newborns in hospital maternity settings. "Whatever the value of the individuals, the man surgeon-midwife is thus going to reign as a master on women's destiny, their intimacy, their choice, their body and supreme power, their capacity to give the life freely"[13] (p. 107).

These authors have shown how men used science and controlled women's exclusive capacity to host and give life. Their scientific knowledge and schematization of women's bodies, specifically the process of procreation, demonstrate how this capacity is enviable for them and has escaped their control for a long time. The uterus is an essential organ of the female body, representing femininity and motherhood. Our interviews with women after hysterectomy or mastectomy have shown how the operation has impacted their physical appearance. The theories on body image mentioned above lead us to consider how this loss has forced them to reorganize and create a new representation of their body. They have used adornment to alternate or compensate.

Throughout this chapter, we have seen how the act of giving shapes the boundaries of psychism. We have seen how women's first experiences of nurturing and handling shape the Ego-Skin and draw the first representation of self at the surface of one's identity. This Ego-Skin associated with body image is built and shaped through mothering techniques, designing ideal social representations of women's image. As these authors have shown, this image is not solely built through one's experience but evolves permanently in contact with others' attention, interactions, and social representations. Breasts and uterus are symbolic female organs holding cultural, social, and erotic importance, and they contribute to women's representation of themselves. Social representations of women are vividly caricatured in tales and folklore, showing dangerous erotic desire for the emancipated devouring mother while paradoxically advertising the character of the benevolent mother. Adornment plays a crucial role in describing them in tales, confirming their personality traits and value as individuals. The analysis of interviews conducted with women after the loss of breasts or uterus confirmed the importance of adornment as a vehicle of narcissistic reconstruction, compensating for the wound. We

---

[13] Translated from original quote in French: "c'est l'homme-médecin qui désormais fonde la sage-femme, qui lui apprend à mettre les enfants au monde, qui la dirige et organise les soins aux mères et aux nouveau-nés, dans les maternités hospitalières. L'homme chirurgien-accoucheur, quelle que soit la valeur des individus, va donc régner en maitre sur le destin des femmes, leur intimité, leur choix, leur corps et, suprême pouvoir, leur capacité à donner librement la vie" (p. 107).

ought to specify that this narcissistic reconstruction process is not to be seen as pathological, but rather as a natural positive coping mechanism where women find personal strength to reinvest themselves as beautiful through adornment. In the following chapters, we will see the specificities of adornment and its symbolism for femininity and motherhood throughout the phases of women's lives. We will discuss its conventional symbolism in rites of passage and personal symbolism in highly disrupting experiences.

References

Anzieu, A. (2005). Propos sur la féminité. *Revue Française de Psychanalyse, 69*, 1103–1116. https://doi.org/10.3917/rfp.694.1103

Anzieu, D. (1995). *Le moi-peau*. Dunod.

Blin, D. (2007). Le lait objet de la rencontre. *Revue française de psychosomatique, 31*, 119–132. https://doi.org/10.3917/rfps.031.0119

Cesbron, P. (2008). Mise au monde et naissance du respect. Dans : Michel Dugnat éd., *Bébés et cultures* (pp. 103–115). Érès. https://doi.org/10.3917/eres.dugna.2008.01.0103

Delaisi de Parseval, G. (2007). Le don du lait. Dans: Dominique Blin éd., *L'allaitement maternel : une dynamique à bien comprendre* (pp. 51–65). Érès. https://doi.org/10.3917/eres.blin.2003.01.0051

Deutsch, H. (1924). *Psychanalyse des fonctions sexuelles chez la femme*. PUF.

Diop, A.-B. (1985). *La famille Wolof, traditions et changements*. Karthala.

Diop, I. S. (2019). *African mythology, femininity, and maternity*. Palgrave Macmillan. https://doi.org/10.1007/978-3-030-24662-4

Dolto, F. (1984). *L'image inconsciente du corps*. Editions du Seuil.

Freud, S. (1967 [1900]). *L'interprétation des rêves*. PUF.

Griaule, M. (1936). *Dieu D'eau, entretiens avec Ogotemmeli*. Fayard.

Gros, C. M. (1983). La relation sexuelle des cancéreuses mastectomisées. *Psychol Med (Paris), 15*(9), 1583–1584.

Lahouati Gérard. Giacomo Casanova : Lana Caprina, Une controverse médicale sur «L 'utérus pensant » à l'Université de Bologne en 1771-1772. Textes établis, introduits et annotés par Paul Mengal, traductions par Roberto Poma, 2000. (Coll. «L'âge des Lumières».). In: Dix-huitième Siècle, n°32, 2000. Le rire, sous la direction de Lise Andries (pp. 592–593). www.persee.fr/doc/dhs_0070-6760_2000_num_32_1_2380_t1_0592_0000_3

Lévi-Strauss, C. (1967). *Les structures élémentaires de la parenté* Mouton de Gruyter, 2002.

Ly, B. (1966). L'honneur et les valeurs morales dans les sociétés ouolof et les toukouleurs du Sénégal, Thèse pour le Doctorat de 3ème cycle en Sociologie. Université de Paris (Unpublished).

Mauss, M. (1950a). Essai sur le don, forme et raison de l'échange dans les sociétés archaïques. In *Sociologie et Anthropologie*. Presses Universitaires de France.

Mauss, M. (1950b). Sixth Part : Les Techniques de Corps. In *Sociologie et Anthropologie*. Presses Universitaires de France.

Parat, H. (2007). Tétons juteux, tétons charnus. *Revue française de psychosomatique, 31*, 9–28. https://doi.org/10.3917/rfps.031.0009

Parat, H. (2011). L'érotique maternelle et l'interdit primaire de l'inceste. *Revue Française de Psychanalyse, 75*, 1609–1614. https://doi.org/10.3917/rfp.755.1609

Rabain, J. (1979). *L'enfant du lignage, Du servage à la classe d'âge*. Payot.

Roux, J. P. (1967). Le lait et le sein dans les traditions turques. *L'Homme, 7*(2), 48–63.

Schilder, P. (1950). *L'image du corps, Étude des forces constructives de la psyché*. Gallimard.

Stork, H. (1986). *Enfances indiennes Etude de Psychologie Transculturelle et comparée du jeune enfant*. Paidos/ Le Centurion.

Ugeux, B. (2006). Perversion de la religion, perversion par la religion. Dans: J. Aïn (Ed.), *Perversions : Aux frontières du trauma* (pp. 207–222). Érès. https://doi.org/10.3917/eres.ain.2006.01.0207

3

The Divine Aspect of Beauty

3.1 Beauty as a Symbol of Purity

3.1.1 From the Cultural Perspective

From this perspective, beauty in tales and mythology, when it describes the pure and benevolent character, refers to simplicity and natural assets. The beautiful character is supposed to be born with this untouched beauty as a natural gift. Youth is also usually an indicator of beauty, as it reflects how intact the girl can be from any interaction with men. Moreover, it represents how she is still the property of a "superior" entity, exempt from any exchange for now. The young and beautiful character is described as a magnificently shaped jewel, reflecting the magnitude of creation.

However, she remains an "unpersonal feminine abstraction" (Von Franz, 1993), and the more she impersonates others' desires, the more she is described as beautiful. As explained in the previous chapter, flexibility and submission to authority are essential qualities in a young girl and truly reflect her suitability for the family's needs.

I. S. Diop, *Adornment, Masquerade and African Femininity*, Pan-African Psychologies,
https://doi.org/10.1007/978-3-031-28748-0_3

In traditional Wolof education, mothers are responsible for their daughters' education, shaping their bodies and minds to be good women in the future. Therefore, the more they are protected from outside influence and contagion, the greater chance they will have to grow as representatives of their mothers' virtue. Hence, they must protect them from bad influence or personal foolishness because beauty and purity are also associated with naivety and innocence, underlining the dangerousness of others as potential corruptors.

Purity contains the idea of being untouched and intact; culturally, in the Wolof culture, it refers to virginity, representing the family's honor in their daughter's marriage. The wedding ceremony and the white color of the bride's clothes show how society expects this moment to demonstrate her purity and congratulate her mother on her excellent education. Even though minds have changed, and people recognize the reality of young women having intimate partners before their weddings, virginity is still highly important.

In other parts of the West African region, purity is not necessarily connected to virginity but solely to youth. For example, we can cite the work of Françoise Héritier (1996) on the Samo people in Burkina Faso, where the first menstruation is the time for a sacrifice, opening access to sexuality for the young woman. The father operating this sacrifice declares that his daughter is now a woman and grants her access to sexuality. This frees her from that superior entity to become a woman of her own and use her body for herself.

There is a link between purity and affiliation and ancestry or divinity, and in this perspective, young women are not available before this act of giving. As Françoise Héritier states (1996, p. 116): "Parents and ancestors' approval is necessary for the girl to enter into sexually active life and then conceive. Therefore, she will not usually be allowed to have sexual intercourse until the rituals and ceremonies of puberty or marriage have been completed for her."[1]

[1] Translated from original quote in French: "L'accord des parents et des ancêtres est nécessaire à la fille, d'abord pour entrer dans une vie active sexuellement, ensuite pour concevoir. Elle n'aura très généralement pas le droit d'avoir des rapports sexuels avant qu'aient été accomplis pour elle les rituels et cérémonies sit de puberté, soit de mariage" (1996, p. 116).

From this stems the idea of transgression when there is intercourse before this moment, since virginity has high importance. Moreover, this idea of purity resides solely in the parents' control of the beginning of their daughter's sexuality. Héritier goes further when she supports the idea that in the Samo culture, a young girl acquires the status of a woman through pregnancy, whether its outcome is a birth or a miscarriage. At this point, she enters society as an autonomous active member. Here again, we can see how the act of giving actualizes her status in society.

On the one hand, beauty, purity, and virginity seem to be the describing qualities of the young female heroine in classic tales. She represents the perfection of creation and the ultimate goal and prize for the male hero, as a reward from divinities for his victory against evil. In this perspective, the heroine only illustrates the hero's fantasy, of a female entity that belongs solely to him and reflects all of his desires.

On the other hand, she represents her parents' integrity and relationship with their ancestry. They have given birth to a daughter, and before her first intercourse, she is under their command and responsibility. Therefore, she only takes her place in the family affiliation when she enters sexuality. The parents' task is to guarantee her integrity and facilitate her transition to another lineage through a sacred alliance. Although her behavior and integrity enhance her beauty, they are more about her reputation and compliance than pure aesthetics.

Furthermore, beauty is highly enhanced in the education of young women to qualify not only their physical appearance but also their behavior. For example, we can cite how body techniques train them for basic movements (salutation, walking, sitting, dancing). These reflect the value of their education and preserve their parents' reputation; they are an inherent part of their training. In West Africa, this training teaches girls to sit, eat, walk, and talk in a specific manner. The reasons for this training include elegance and politeness (Diop, 1985).

For all these body techniques, beauty reflects good education and wisdom, and thus, purity. Thus, purity is not only what comes naturally to the girl as a reflection of divinity, symbolizing youth and creation, but also a social construction enforced by shaping and teaching. In other words, the young girl comes with inner beauty and purity offered by ancestry and divine authority, and then her parents' role is to shape that raw jewel into a social construct, adaptable to society. Only under this format can she see her status evolve from girl to woman.

In the Wolof culture of Senegal, we can observe the symbolism of the ritual bath (Diop, 1985, 2011). The *bajjën* (paternal aunt) operates this crucial part of the wedding ritual, and she bathes her niece in a bathtub into which she puts silver jewels, a kola nut, and some specific plants. Muslims may also add a verse of the Quran written by a marabout on a piece of paper to protect and bless the bride. On this occasion, the *bajjën* initiates and advises her niece about marriage and sexuality. Finally, after the first wedding night, there is the *Laaban* ceremony, where the virginal loincloth shown to the whole village proves the purity of the young bride (Diop, 2011).

We can analyze this ritual scene as a rebirth of the young woman. Recalling the traditional baptism, naming the child, and integrating them in the family lineage, this new ritual bath disconnects the woman from her lineage to give her away to her husband's family. The sacrificial elements remaining in the bathtub are presents for the ancestors granting her exit. Each offering symbolizes a specific wish for her new life as it is repaid to her ancestors. Dressed in a specific fabric provided by her in-laws, she dies in her family to be reborn in her husband's and changes affiliation to become part of a new lineage. This union is sealed after the *Laaban*, where her virginity is proof of her untouched nature. This second ceremony tends to be forgotten and replaced by a formal conversation between the husband and his mother-in-law or the daughter's maternal representative to thank her for her excellent education and testify for her daughter's purity. The opposite would be considered highly shameful to both the bride and her family and raise doubts about their suitability as parents.

Purity, in this perspective, is given, preserved, and shown as the symbol of a parent's virtue and sense of duty. Beauty appears in global behavior through gesture and speech. It starts with a natural gift but resides beyond physical advantages. In fact, in the descriptions of young feminine figures in tales, their grace and finesse are clear indicators of how their beauty echoes their inner purity and delicacy. Girls' education reinforces this ideal version of the fresh, pure, delicate girl, untouched and out of reach from improper influences. The family is responsible for raising her to the best of their abilities to avoid future misbehavior and shame. Although society evolves, and people have fewer prejudices in the present time, the worst situation expected for families is teenage pregnancy because virginity is socially representative as proof of the girl's integrity, honesty, and honor. A bride's former sexual experience can be perceived as threatening as it may underline competition and rivalry between her husband and her previous lovers. One can assume that it is more comfortable for men to feel that they are their wives' only point of comparison, as other men's performances would make them feel insecure. Here we can think of Devereux's idea (1965) about exogamy and women's exchange as a relationship between men themselves.

In the next section, we will discuss the religious perspective of beauty as a symbol of purity.

3.1.2 From the Religious Perspective

Beauty in the creation reflects the immensity of the Creator's power. In the religious perspective, the genesis emphasizes the perfection of nature as an actual divine creation. One example of this perfection is the image of the Garden of Eden as the perfect place, but the original sin introduces imperfection in this creation. Humanhood is driven out of this Paradise because of the impossibility for perfection to host such imperfect creatures. Hence, they are doomed to live in this world, suffering from everything that makes them human, their sins, fears, and pains. These unpleasant things are explained paradoxically to perfection for an answer to the question: If we are one among all perfect creations, why do we experience this? Is this not proof of imperfection? The answer may be that the Creator has chosen to make us suffer through this as a punishment for the original sin.

However, there are still ways to achieve perfection in our different religions, sometimes through prayer and sometimes through sacrifice and chastity. In Islam and Christianity, believers can acquire a clearer vision of divine perfection through prayer and unconditional faith. In Islam, the exercise of religion requires purity, through ritual purification prior to every prayer, to clear body and soul of mental and physical impurities before facing the Creator. This ritualization through water purifies the believer with the same intention to purify each individual for ritual ceremonies (baptism, wedding, and death). Furthermore, it seems that water has the power to erase and give a new beginning, the newness implicitly synonymous with purity. In this dimension, purity in the religious perspective joins the meaning of this concept in the cultural perspective. It echoes the sense of newness close to the Creator as if it were a return to a blank page before the original sin.

Moreover, religions also provide guidelines for relationships between men, women, and children. They codify the systems of alliance, and especially women's interactions with men. In this frame, integrity and virginity are tied to the concept of purity.

The image of perfection, beauty, and purity in the religious perspective is different from one religion to another and mainly depends on the cultural environment where they were revealed. Perfection and beauty reside in Islam's honest faith and ethical religious practice. Purity does not refer to long-term chastity; sexuality is only recognized and approved in the context of marriage. According to Boudhiba (1975), sexuality, when lived within the limits of a marriage, is supposed to demonstrate the Creator's heavenly pleasures.

Perfection means being as close as possible to the prophetic life, a true believer, fair and honest to his family and followers. Members of the prophetic family are also represented as symbols of perfection, as they are described as wise, honest, and scrupulously respectful of religious rules. Hence, in Islam, the Creator is and remains out of reach for believers; they are invited to follow the example of his prophet and may be rewarded in the afterlife when they graciously enter heaven.

Nonetheless, this vision differs from one religion to another. Perfection and purity may not be compatible with sexuality in other religions. Humans' incapacity to refrain from their desires and obey the Creator's rules has caused the end of that heavenly beginning and terminated the original perfection. Sins are the manifestations of their imperfection and are divided into categories to reflect the plurality of human flaws. Religious codes are created to prevent humans from falling into their sins and force to them to refrain from their incorrect impulses.

There can be an association between sexuality and sins or human flaws, promoting an image of purity and beauty to represent the woman who has never sinned. Virginity is a symbol of her perfection and hence the religious image of the virgin woman who gave birth to the purest human, closest to the Creator. He chose her for her innocence and the beauty of her soul. We can see how beauty is present in Christianity, demonstrating the link between purity, virginity, and sacredness.

Women are closer to the Creator in their purest state, so young women are pure because they represent this specific connection. Moreover, virgins are considered even more divine in Islam as they are supposed to be the ones welcoming pious men upon their arrival in heaven.

Virginity is as sacred as heaven and distinguishes pure women from regular ones, vulgarized in the cycle of exchange. The saint trinity represents a family marked by the divine presence of the Creator. Saint Mary is the purest woman who gave birth to the purest man without losing her virginity to sexuality. She is the incarnation of perfection in Christianity, a role model for individuals willing to get closer to the Creator through chastity and religious ethics.

Saint Mary is a mother and no longer a woman. She has elevated herself to this stage, showing courage, passion, and faith. She is the actual image of motherhood, detached from her womanly nature, and remains in the collective unconscious as the benevolent mother, detached from the seductive, tempting, and hazardous nature of femininity.

To illustrate this connection between the idea of the virgin mother and the Creator, Liliane Abensour describes the maternal as follows: "the maternal is at the same time creator and creation, origin and manufacture, essence and existence"[2] (2011, p. 1335). Michèle Bertrand developed the representation and the divine character granted to the maternal with the examples of the ancient Egyptian religion and modern Catholicism. These two authors underline the connection between the woman who gives birth to a child and thus gives life and the Creator of humanity. This connection also induces the idea of the maternal omnipotence and the archaic mother.

In society and the religious perspective, the process of procreation is encouraged in the marital relationship, suggesting that this is the purpose

[2] Translated from original quote in French: "le maternel est tout à la fois créateur et création, origine et fabrique, essence et existence."

of the latter institution: granting regulated access to parenting. Although it implies the loss of virginity, this necessary exchange promotes a divine intervention in the process of child conception and childbirth since the union is recognized and validated by religious authorities.

Furthermore, the intervention of authorities in the marital relationship induces the idea of them not being men and women facing each other, but rather individuals acting under supervision. This representation might imply images and social roles. Religious codes tend to improve us, making us able to refrain from our urges and bringing culture to our animal impulsive nature. Purity is either this state of virginity without the pollution of impulses or the ability to resolve this nature and become superior to humanhood, approaching divinity.

Hence the woman representing divine beauty and purity must master her impulses and stop herself from giving in to desire and lust. Religious principles and practices contain guidelines on this matter and threats for dissuasion. Being a pure and divine woman in the religious representation means to elevate oneself above impulses.

3.1.3 From the Psychoanalytical Perspective

In *La Vie Sexuelle* (1918), Freud returns to the notion of taboo, introducing the taboo of virginity, which he associates with that of menstruation. This author wrongly and ethnocentrically calls a person from a culture outside of urban or European frames a "primitive," and according to him this person cannot separate the enigmatic phenomenon of menstrual flow from sadistic representations. He interprets menstruation, at least the first menstruation, as the bite of a supernatural animal and perhaps as the sign of a sexual relationship with this entity. In this sense, the girl is taboo insofar as she is supposedly the property of a superior entity: the founding ancestor. According to Freud, the woman is taboo, not only in particular situations that arise from sexual life (menstruation, pregnancy, childbirth) but beyond this, as relations with them are also subject to substantial restrictions.

Then, later in his work, Freud evoked the difficulties of psychoanalysis in analyzing an adult woman's sexual life, which he qualified as a "dark continent" (1925, p. 31). This formulation supposedly underlines the enigmatic character of women in psychoanalysis and raises questions about the reason for these prohibitions. However, we ought to note its possible reference to sexual fantasies related to the actual black continent.

Assoun, in his work (1983), revisits Freud's studies on women. According to this author, Freud distinguishes the sacred and the seductive woman, and men dissociate these two figures. Their sexual impulses cannot be driven toward a woman who is a maternal figure, because it revives the Oedipus complex. Their incestual fantasies are diverted to a more seductive woman, impersonating femininity. The maternal figure preserves this sacred representation, her intact and untouchable nature. Assoun (1983) evokes the idea of the fatal woman in Freudian symbolism. She makes men anxious because she represents a threat based on the fatality she herself undergoes by the effect of *Kultur*. In this conception, femininity and maternity are closely linked because, according to this author, femininity is nothing less than the phallic expression of the power to create life.

Later, in the second part of this chapter, we will see that the maternal figure also incarnates death, leading us to discuss her more aggressive features.

Claude Lévi-Strauss (1967) and Georges Devereux (1965) were more interested in women's status in the exchange cycle and men's communication. They are the object of the two primary rules that structure society and are subject to specific restrictions. Moreover, because of women's importance in the structure of society, rules of alliance codify the relationship between men and their access to women. Women can then sometimes appear as inaccessible and forbidden, and can be the source of fantasies.

Religious and mythological figures are archetypes, incarnating unconscious fantasies and fears. We can see in the maternal figure our representation of the Paradise, intact and enveloping, full of everything we could desire, and inaccessible to our reach. The maternal figure wears this pure beauty, celestial and divine, dissociated from sexuality, close to our representation of perfection in the religious dimension.

To understand this dissociation, we can draw on the theories of Melanie Klein (1957) on the construction of psychism. According to this author, psychism starts its construction from birth, and the natural impulses are primary features, preexisting any mental structure. From birth, we enter the conflict between life and death impulses, and our ego results from this conflict.

Defense mechanisms of introjection and projection actively build the preforms of the psychic apparatus, the objects, and the Ego:

- Good experiences (satisfaction, gratification) are associated with life impulses (libidinal impulses). The baby introjects and integrates the pleasant feeling as a fragment of a good object, being the base of the first fragmented but internal Ego. Good experiences constitute the Ego.
- Bad experiences (frustration, displeasure, or pain) are associated with death impulses. The mechanism of projection acts defensively and expulses them outside. This process leads to the construction of an aggressive feeling with a fragment of object rejected in the non-Ego. Therefore, a dangerous, persecuting object arises: the archaic maternal superego; everything functions in a dichotomous mode (Ego/non-Ego, Introjection/Projection, Good/Bad). The Ego is a good gratifying object inside the baby. He idealizes it and must preserve it.

Klein's theory describes how defensive mechanisms such as cleavage, introjection, and projection support this dissociation. The good maternal imago is integrated into the Ego, while the bad maternal imago acts as a threatening destructive authoritarian figure of an archaic maternal superego. The representation of the good maternal imago retains the fantasies of perfection, wholeness, and beauty.

It is apparent that the maternal image's perfection and beauty reflect primary fantasies of early experiences, explaining this attachment to its sacredness.

Yolande Govindama (2006) has studied female deities' representation in Hinduism. She has explored the universe of the Goddess Petiaye, also called Karteri. Petiaye is the goddess of birth and pregnancy; women trying to conceive and until the birth of their baby have a sacrificial cult to observe. Petiaye/ Karteri is an ambivalent figure, representing a good and protective mother and, simultaneously, a destructive and murderous force. She is represented as powerful and beautiful in poems, songs, and statues. The following poem describes invocations to her[3] (Govindama, 2006, p. 93):

- The mother goddess, Karteri, the mother;
- You, in a state of mortification, the mother, come;
- You the mother of Mouttouyroulan (popular god), the mother goddess;
- The hatchet, the mother, your beautiful teeth;
- The red hair, the mother, the beauty of your hair;
- Red with anger, the merciful mother, the beauty of your face;
- First egg, the mother, first chicken;
- Dressed in Kandagni (Indian cloth), the mother, a corset for you;
- The gentle mother, there is a red sari for you;
- The protective mother, there is a corset for you.

This invitation prayer to the goddess offers colored clothes as welcoming gifts: the red color is for Karteri, and the black color (symbolizing protection) is for Petiaye. Kleinian ambivalence is repeated in this figure, elevating the mother to the level of divinity while fearing her power. This anxiety toward this power seems so archaic that it has retained this dissociation resulting in this ambivalent figure. We can see how adornment symbolizes this ambivalence of the goddess' two avatars.

The following section will discuss the other part of this ambivalent figure: the devious and threatening mother. We will explore how, in this figure, beauty is a different concept, far from purity and closer to sin.

---

[3] Translated from original quote in French:

- La déesse mère, Karteri, la mère;
- Vous, en état de mortification, la mère, venez;
- Vous la mère de Mouttouyroulan (dieu populaire), la déesse mère;
- La hachette, la mère, vos belles dents;
- La chevelure rousse, la mère, la beauté de votre chevelure;
- Rouge de colère, la mère clémente, la beauté de votre visage;

  Premier oeuf, la mère, première poule;
- Vêtue de Kandagni (tissu indien), la mère, un corset pour vous;
- La mère douce, il y a un sari rouge pour vous;
- La mère protectrice, il y a un corset pour vous.

3.2 Beauty as a Symbol of Malevolence

3.2.1 The Devouring Mother

This figure is emblematic of an all-powerful female entity. Some of the devouring mother's representations are beautiful, and seduction is one of her best assets to deceive and trap men. The example of Mami Wata is illustrative of how beauty echoes her malevolence. She is attractive and has much power to grant money and achievement. These facilitations are illusions because she has the power to take them away as she pleases. Men attracted by money and lust gain these privileges. They are abandoning the values of family and honesty to become servants of their greed and lies. Southern Africa has another figure similar to Mami Wata. She is described as a mermaid who requires human sacrifice to maintain her servant's privileges. In this case, we can observe a link between economic success and abandonment of family values, implying that men, desperate for power, would risk and sacrifice everything for it. The first sacrifice they make is their family's trust when they seal this secret contract. Then, they put them in danger, as prey for this entity insatiable for life and flesh. Finally, they show this idea of false comprehension of a situation where they can never win but still think they are in control.

Beauty, for the devouring mother, is a trick and an illusion. In some tales, she can change forms and attract her victims using the traits of a beautiful young woman. When she is defeated, she loses this power and assumes her original form, where her ugliness transcribes her wickedness. Here, the moral of the story reinstates the principle of reality to replace this former order, where she lives by the principle of pleasure, using magic to take everything she wants. This character describes not only insatiability but also a distortion of reality to incarnate her fantasies. She represents a part of each human, in our attempts to desperately realize our fantasies of all-powerfulness at every cost.

Furthermore, in their exaggerated forms, lust and greed, as they characterize the devouring mother, represent men's insatiability. Hence, we can say that this entity is an emphasis on men's faults and weaknesses. She incarnates their flaws to make a customized trap.

In some tales, the figure of the devouring mother also attracts women, but the seduction process is more like an influence. The figure seduces women with her power and drags them into the path of emancipation from men's domination. Moreover, this vision of emancipation implies the idea of sacrifice from women to this entity, emphasizing the idea of incompatibility between professional or social achievement and family life. Although seduction techniques and beauty are part of women's legitimately recognized qualities for men, they are not positive when they appear too bright or uncontrolled because they induce the idea that phallic power is on their side. Therefore, every movement evoking the figure of the devouring mother is dangerous and requires extra attention in the process of education.

Veronique Tadjo (2005), in her description of Abraha Pokou,[4] describes her effect on women:

> The goddess's seduction was complete, limitless. Nobody could resist her. Women she approached succumbed to her extraordinary beauty, stunned by her perfect presence. Moreover, after having known them, she disappeared forever, distraught with grief, leaving her companions in an immense, inconsolable nostalgia. They stopped all activity to look for her, walking with a determined step, running here and there, until they collapsed out of fatigue. One often found them alone, naked and curled up on the ground.

This description shows the marginalization of women who are victims of her charms. Following her order causes the victim to lose total control of herself, mind and body. Although the consequences are nearly the same for men, we can see this threat as a warning for women to stay on the path of social rules. The devouring mother's influence can only drive her victim to marginalization. Nevertheless, society makes sure to realize

[4]Translated from original quote in French: "La séduction de la déesse était entière, sans limites. Personne ne pouvait lui résister. Les femmes dont elle s'approchait succombaient également à son extraordinaire beauté, étourdies par sa présence parfaite. Et quand, après les avoir connues, elle disparaissait pour toujours, ses compagnes, éperdues de chagrin, étaient prises d'une nostalgie immense, inconsolable. Elles cessaient toute activité pour se mettre à sa recherche, marchant d'un pas déterminé, courant ici et là, jusqu'à s'écrouler de fatigue. On les retrouvait le plus souvent seules dénudées et recroquevillées sur le sol" (Tadjo, 2005, p. 50).

this self-fulfilling prophecy because it sets effective rules to marginalize women stepping out of the line. Emancipation, sometimes a trait of malevolence, can induce defiance and calumnious interpretations, contributing to marginalization.

When describing a man, lust is supposedly a weakness, but for a woman, it is a fault and a weapon against men, society, and education. Representations like this carry the implicit idea that women deserve to be punished for their sins and serve as a basis for explanations and excuses for gender-based violence. Some women themselves would support this idea when justifying this kind of violence. Emancipation and independence are sometimes excuses and explanations for violence because they change the order of things and imply disruption. From that point, since they have created a disorder, women are responsible for the consequences.

Furthermore, in tales, this idea of disorder and chaos in a world dominated by the figure of a devouring mother is the reason for all calamities. The devouring mother is limitless and subjects all men to her power, enslaving them to their desire. Her beauty is their flaw, and they cannot resist her demands. This legendary picture is very similar to the Freudian Myth of the primal horde,[5] except that the destructive, tyrannical authority is a woman. In this myth, the hero has to kill the tyrannical authority to reinstate balance. Education repeats this exercise of eliminating the devouring mother in each woman, yet some reminiscence survives of this process.

Women's education enhances the determinism of their suffering. They are responsible for whatever happens to them and cannot blame others for their situation. The concept of *Ndey-Ju-liggey* translates this determinism of cause and effect. It does not promote values of respect, nor does it explain the reasons for others' malevolence. This concept only promises a good ending for those who accept suffering while implicitly threatening those who do not. The character of the devouring mother is the exact opposite of the *Ndey-Ju-liggey*. She expresses strong emotions and reacts

[5] "A violent and jealous father [...] keeps all of the females for himself and drives away his sons as they grow up. [...] One day the brothers who have been driven out came together, killed and devoured their father and so made an end of the patriarchal horde. [This] was the beginning of so many things—of social organization, of moral restrictions and of religion."

selfishly, disregarding the consequences. Here again, we observe a contradiction between pleasure and reality principles. *Ndey-Ju-liggey* incarnates the work of society and culture to tame the devouring mother in her and reduce her power. However, the devouring mother remains vivid in the common unconscious as a frightening but attractive figure. In the next section, we will discuss this ambivalence.

3.2.2 Envy and Ambivalence

Melanie Klein gave considerable importance to the concept of envy (1957):

> Envy plays a role in the desire to seize the attributes of the opposite sex and take over or deteriorate those of the same-sex parent. Thus, in the positive or negative oedipal situation, jealousy and paranoid rivalry appear in both sexes, however different their evolution, and find their origin in the excessive Envy of the original object, the mother, or rather the maternal breast.[6] (p. 46)

The myth of Caroweelo, in the Horn of Africa region (Ismaël, 2011), refers to an ancient queen or warlord who dominated a kingdom in the Abyssinian region for several decades. The myth emphasizes her practice of emasculating men around her, especially her two sons in charge of her camel's livestock. She is the founder of this region because, after her defeat, her body parts spread all over the country, forming mountains and hills in the landscape. According to Ismaël (2011), the name Caroweelo can be deconstructed into *Caro*, meaning land, and *Weelo*, the name of the people living in this region. Her grandson defeated her, trained by her husband, his grandfather, known to be the cleverest man. Her ruthlessness and thirst for power are opposed to her husband's cleverness and love for their grandson. They have defeated her because they

[6] "L'envie joue un rôle dans le désir de s'emparer des attributs du sexe opposé, ainsi que de s'approprier ou de détériorer ceux du parent de même sexe. Ainsi dans la situation œdipienne positive ou négative la jalousie et la rivalité paranoïde apparaissent dans les deux sexes, aussi différente que soit leur évolution, et trouvent leur origine dans l'envie excessive à l'objets originel, la mère, ou plutôt le sein maternel" (Klein, 1957, p. 46).

knew her weaknesses and thus allowed all men to take back their power and masculinity.

Historians have identified a queen in the history of the Agaw people from the Abyssinian region, who reigned for thirty years. Due to her gender, people from the neighboring kingdoms referred to her subjects as emasculated, suggesting that men must be lesser to accept being ruled by a queen for so many years. Historians have connected the figure of Caroweelo to this queen and analyzed the similarity between them, concluding that Caroweelo is a mythical representation of this queen who existed in real history. This character is so important in the region's history that the male descendants of her people are still called "the emasculated." Some authors have focused on the process of emasculation, as explained in the myth, and suggested that it might have been a "mental castration" rather than a literal one (Ismael, 2011).

Here we can see a clear link between power and gender. This queen could reign "like a man," and her rule lasted approximately thirty years, which suggests extraordinary diplomatic and strategic skills. However, the emasculated status of her subjects remains the most notable point in the legend, drawing our attention to the idea of her seizing their masculinity simply by taking power and retaining it.

This emphasis on sexual organs leads us to discuss Bruno Bettleheim's position on female circumcision. This practice exists in the Horn of Africa region.

Bettelheim (1954) concludes that female circumcision has been imposed on girls by men (p. 172). The author notes that if the girl "sometimes desires to be cut, it is not because of the modification of her organ, but because this mutilation gives her a higher social status or is a prerequisite for marriage"[7] (p. 172). Bettelheim first suggests that the infliction of female genital mutilation is a way for men to take revenge on women for their resentment of their fertility. Later, the author withdraws this idea as unsound and argues that excision is a "male attempt to gain

[7] Translated from original quote in French: "de désirer l'excision, ce n'est pas en raison de la modification apportée à son organe, mais parce que cette mutilation lui confère un statut social plus élevé ou est une condition préalable indispensable au mariage" (p. 172).

control over female sexual functions"[8] (p. 174). It would thus be motivated by the man's envy of female sexual functions. Through excision, "the male is satisfied with a symbolic order that he can give to the external female genitalia, without influencing the woman's fertility or sexual pleasure. (…) By all these acts, men try to convince themselves, and women with them, of their positive contribution to fertility"[9] (p. 175). Finally, Bettelheim refers to the possible reciprocity of this practice by the fact that circumcision, in many Australian tribes, is initiated by women, showing the envy of the human being, in front of the other sex, and "the desire to acquire the power and control, of the other's genital apparatus"[10] (p. 178).

The envy toward the other gender relates to Melanie Klein's idea of this archaic drive to introject the primary object. In the myth of Caroweelo, we can imagine a connection between the distribution of power and the role of a queen-mother. Although her position grants her all-powerfulness and every man's dreams, her gender makes her socially unfit for this position and allows them to claim the power to install their idea of balance. The husband's figure in the myth acts as a third party in her relationship with her children, and his mission is to use his cleverness to save them. Despite the length of her rule, implying her people's loyalty, her defeat seems to be acclaimed by all. This myth of an original, unhappy, and unbalanced family, and the hero who gave birth to the landscape and the society, replays an Oedipal tale of how the phallus was taken from the mother's hand to be given to the grandson and men in general.

In this Oedipean history, the mother uses her power to castrate her sons and mentally emasculate her husband. Her daughter holds the key to ending their misery because she can give birth to a son. Here, women, in opposition to men, have control over sexuality. Because they are not castrated, they generate envy on the male's side. The Oedipus complex

[8] Translated from original quote in French: "tentative mâle d'acquérir le contrôle des fonctions sexuelles féminines" (p. 174).

[9] "…le mâle se contente d'un ordre symbolique qu'il peut donner aux organes génitaux féminins externes, sans influencer la fécondité de la femme ni son plaisir sexuel. (…) Par tous ces actes, les hommes essayent de se convaincre, et les femmes avec eux, de leur contribution positive à la fécondité" (p. 175).

[10] "…le désir d'acquérir le pouvoir et le contrôle, de l'appareil génital de l'autre" (p. 178).

takes place between the daughter and the father, united against the mother, using the grandson as bait. The love she has for her grandson, being her flaw, underlines the fact that, after all, she remains a woman, sensitive to a child's trick and charm.

This myth highlights two aspects:

- Society views women in positions of power as dangerous.
- Men under their power feel castrated.

Thus, we can imagine that the feeling of envy is the basis for the relations of power between the genders. Each wants to appropriate the phallus and uses strategies to obtain it. Beauty in powerful and devouring female characters demonstrates their power, phallus, and authority. Their power lies in their accessories and adornment as proof of their wealth. For the character of Mami Wata, it is illusory, but for queen Caroweelo, it is genuinely her wealth as a leader. These accessories are phallic attributes of power, echoing their omnipotence and fueling men's envy, taking them back to this archaic Kleinian representation of the primary mother, source of the maternal superego.

Adornment, in this perspective, retains a significant meaning because it sends a message to the viewer. Women can incarnate one figure or the other on a beauty spectrum ranging from a maternal, virginal extreme to a seductive, feminine one. They navigate on this spectrum, as they do in imaginary social representations. The myth of Petiaye/Karteri has shown how they can raise ambivalence, alternatively incarnating both extremes, through the description of their adornment.

In the next section, we will dive further into psychoanalytic representations to understand better the concepts of female taboo and women's connection to earth, land, and nature.

3.2.3 Man Versus Nature

Ordinary and traditional language associates women with nature and versatility. In tales, we have seen how the Sun is representative of the male gender, while the Moon is representative of the female gender (Von Franz,

1993). Moreover, the Moon's changes during the month evoke the female gynecological cycle, reinforcing this resemblance. This connection justifies the idea that women are hesitant and undecided, yet their education prioritizes flexibility and adaptation. However, they are historically known to be responsible for men's bad decision-making. They induce temptation and make them unable to resist their charms. This paradoxical representation of women also reflects their unpredictability, like the Moon.

Women are part of nature, and as such, are pictured as instinctive and impulsive. Every female character described in the previous section is connected to nature:

- Mami Wata lives in the water.
- Caroweelo is attached to the East African land.
- Ndjeddo Dewal is created from plants and animals.

They all incarnate men's fear of natural forces, over which they have no control. Following Freud's (1958) work on the taboo of femininity, Jacqueline Schaeffer also mentions the prohibitions linked to the menstruating woman and the anxieties attached to it. "The menstruating woman, says the author, destroys all that she is supposed to protect and produce as mother earth, she destroys life, as she destroys the child that she does not carry"[11] (2005, p. 15–16). The author sees behind the taboo of blood the fear inspired by the dark forces of life and death, that of an archaic mother all-powerful and devouring, possessing the exclusive right to give life and take it back. Furthermore, the taboo of menstrual blood binds together the desire to remain in contact with the original maternal bond to maintain this fusion out of reach, thus participating in the general taboo of incest (2005, p. 22). Indeed, according to this author, blood could be considered metaphorically as the mark of women's connection to earth and nature, and thus their belonging to a maternal and/or

[11] Translated from original quote in French: "La femme menstruée, dit l'auteur, détruit tout ce qu'elle est censée protéger et produire en tant que terre-mère, elle détruit la vie, comme elle détruit l'enfant qu'elle ne porte pas."

supernatural higher power. Therefore, because of this, they are not freely accessible, and the limitations are ramifications of the general taboo of incest.

Hence, with this representation of women, we will explore the concept of femininity and its connection with adornment and masquerade.

Catherine Delarue (2004) distinguishes femininity, feminine, and the woman. According to this author, "femininity is particularly related to the imaginary, the feminine, to the symbolic about the feminine gender of grammar and language, and the woman is related to the Real in the Lacanian sense of the term, insofar as she does not exist as a category of the universal"[12] (p. 62). She is interested in a woman's position as an object of man's desire. According to her, the woman as such object fills a lack by occupying this place, which she can only take by identifying herself with the phallus. Indeed, as submissive to the phallic signifier, she is brought to be in a position of answering to the man's lack, and in this perspective, to impersonate the phallus, allowing herself to avoid the Freudian dialectic. "It is the man's glance, on this desired object, coveted, that allows the woman to escape her anxiety of the phallic lack. The woman seems to be captured by the look that she arouses. If femininity is a fantasy, it is solicited only by the male's spurred desire, magnetized by the feminine masquerade"[13] (p. 69).

Therefore, femininity exists in the man's glance, like a set of elements, calling to a man's imagination and desire. Femininity pushes a woman to put herself in a position to mirror it, while masking what in herself causes fear. She is using this femininity as a masquerade to protect them from what she hides.

Schaeffer focuses on describing femininity in its relationship with the female genitalia. Although according to this author, femininity is visible, it is in harmony with the phallic logic, to which it answers in echo. The

[12] Translated from original quote in French: "la féminité relèverait particulièrement de l'imaginaire, le féminin, du symbolique en référence au genre féminin de la grammaire et du langage, et la femme relèverait du réel au sens lacanien du terme, c'est-à-dire en tant qu'elle n'existe pas comme une catégorie de l'universel."

[13] Translated from original quote in French: "C'est le regard de l'homme, sur cet objet désiré, convoité, qui permet à la femme d'échapper elle aussi à l'angoisse du manque phallique. La femme semble captée par le regard qu'elle suscite. Si la féminité est un fantasme, celui-ci n'est sollicité par le désir masculin qui est aiguillonné, aimanté, parce que l'on peut nommer la mascarade féminine."

role of femininity is to value what is seen and shown, to reassure against the fear of castration in men and women. According to her, what causes this fear is the woman's genitalia and menstrual blood. "It is regarding this fear for their gender, that girls and women use femininity. The femininity of the surface, that of the parade, the masquerade, the dresses, heels, etc.... (...) If men's narcissistic overinvestment relates to the penis, it is their whole body that girls and women can invest like a phallic whole, hung to the reassurance of the relationship with the other"[14] (p. 9).

To conclude this chapter, we can state that women's movements on the beauty spectrum transcribe ambivalent feelings of humanity toward their gender. Historically, culturally, and religiously, adornment is codified by gender. Nevertheless, as Schaeffer notes, adornment refers to more than clothes or jewels and disguises the whole female body to mirror attention and anxiety. Body techniques are one of the tools of this masquerade, magnetizing men's glance. Women are taught to master them, and are trained to avoid showing resemblance to extreme feminine figures. In this perspective, adornment expresses not only a woman's status, but also culture and social class. Whatever their limitations and social rules, as much as they can use adornment as masquerade, they can also use it as a vehicle for their own expression.

In the next chapter, we will explore adornment specificities, and symbolism in certain situations like rituals and in general as a code to recognize social classes.

References

Abensour, L. (2011). L'ombre du maternel, Extraits remis par Josette Garon. *Revue française de psychanalyse, 75*(5), 1297–1335.

Assoun, P.-L. (1983). *Freud et la femme*. Édition Payot.

Bettelheim, B. (1954). *Les blessures symboliques*. Gallimard, 1971.

[14]Translated from original quote in French: "C'est en regard de cette angoisse pour leur féminin que les filles et les femmes ont recours à la féminité. Féminité de surface, celle de la parade, ou de la mascarade, celle des robes, talons, etc.... (...) Si le surinvestissement narcissique des hommes porte sur le pénis, c'est leur corps tout entier que les filles et les femmes peuvent investir comme tout phallique, accroché à la réassurance du rapport de l'autre."

Bouhdiba, A. (1975). *La sexualité en Islam.*
Delarue, C. (2004). La féminité est-elle un fantasme ? *Analyse freudienne Presse, 2*(10), 61–73.
Devereux, G. (1965). Ethnopsychanalyse complémentariste, chap. *4 : La Notion de Parenté.* Flammarion.
Diop, A.-B. (1985). *La famille Wolof, traditions et changements.* Karthala.
Diop, I. (2011). *Le Sénégal, in Temps et rites de passage, Naissance, enfance, culture et religion*, dir. By Yolande Govindama (pp. 21–39). Edition Karthala.
Freud, S. (1918). Le tabou de la virginité. In *La Vie Sexuelle.*
Freud, S. (1958). *Totem and Taboo: Some Points of Agreement between the Mental Lives of Savages and Neurotics* (p. 103).
Govindama, Y. (2006). *Le monde hindou à La Réunion, une approche anthropologique et psychanalytique.* Karthala (p. 96).
Héritier, F. (1996). *Masculin/Féminin I. La pensée de la différence.* Odile Jacob, Septembre 2012.
Ismael, A. M. (2011). Chapter 6: Caroweelo, aux origines du Mythe, in *Traversées, histoire et mythes de Djibouti,* dir. By Chiré & Ndagano. Revue de l'Université de Djibouti, Karthala.
Klein, M. (1957). *Envie et gratitude et autres essais.* Éditions Gallimard, 1968.
Lévi-Strauss, C. (1967). *Les structures élémentaires de la parenté.* Mouton &Co and Maison des Sciences de l'Homme.
Schaeffer, J. (2005). Le fil rouge du sang de la femme. *Champ psychosomatique, 4*(40), 39–64.
Tadjo, V. (2005). Abraha Pokou, Actes Sud.
Von Franz, M.-L. (1993). *La femme dans les contes de fées*, 1972, Éditions Albin Michel.

4

Adornment and Symbolism

Adornment is as social and global as it is personal. Previously, we have discussed that the representation of women and adornment can convey connotations of good or evil archetypes. In that frame, we have introduced concepts of body image and Ego-Skin to underline how this representation is imprinted since birth through body techniques and education.

We have seen how these means undermine feminine malevolence, as caricatured by cultural examples told in storytelling. Through analyzing various authors' writing on the topic of feminine duality, we have observed how the ambivalence of the relationship toward femininity transpires through these caricatures. What appears to be the intersection of two representations, seductive and protective, is a spectrum where women move throughout their lives and impulses.

In this chapter, we will focus on the nature and specificities of adornment. We will draw to Mauss's work on the gift to understand the meaning of rituals, and we will focus on the symbolism of ritual clothes and accessories. The analysis of their symbolism will enlighten us on their role and origin. Indeed, we will identify their origin as being as ambivalent as those feminine representations. The Others, Maternal Other and Great

I. S. Diop, *Adornment, Masquerade and African Femininity*, Pan-African Psychologies,
https://doi.org/10.1007/978-3-031-28748-0_4

Other, will be remembered as the principal givers and absent masters of ritualistic ceremonies, forcing subjects to repetitively renew their affiliation to their lineage and marking the ambivalence between their natural fusional impulses and the law of the Other.

The relationship to jewelry remains connected to narcissism, and we will prove this by discussing historical sources on adornment in West Africa. We will see how personal adornment can allow one to claim or show self-valorization.

First, we will discuss ritual adornment and its symbolism to understand and identify the forces at work in stating the rules of women's aesthetics. Then, we will go through history and anthropological literature to observe the link between adornment and social hierarchy. Finally, we will discuss the symbolism of jewelry and gold.

4.1 Adornment and Rituals

4.1.1 Rites of Passage

Yolande Govindama (2006, 2011) has studied rites of passage in La Réunion (French Island in the Indian Ocean) and analyzed their symbolism. She draws on Van Gennep's (1909) work to define and describe them. Rites of passage, according to Van Gennep (1909), are rites of symbolic separation punctuating the different psychobiological stages of the subject, from birth to death. During the time of the ritual, the subject goes through three stages:

- a preliminary phase where the subject is separated from the group and isolated.
- then the margin or liminary phase where the subject is neither in the previous stage nor in the superior stage. They are anchored in the mythical time and the sacred space of the ritual of which they must be impregnated as much on the bodily level (marking, involving all senses, etc.) as on the mental level (focusing, learning of the myth,

initiation, memorial encoding of the state of the margin to forge the identity).
- and finally, the last phase, where the subject is reintegrated into the group with their new status.

There are different types of rites, and they cover all decisive parts of the subject's life (pregnancy and birth, childhood, engagement and wedding, and finally, funeral rites).

According to Govindama (2006, p. 13), these rites guarantee the unity of body and soul, from conception or birth, until death. These rites remind the subject, at each stage of life, of their human condition as a mortal being. They have the purpose of recognizing and managing death anxiety. The illusion of an afterlife through the belief in soul immortality renders death more bearable.

Indeed, according to Freud (1915), no one can have a representation of their death because this is irrepresentable in the unconscious.

But by intervening at the very beginning of life, these rites also introduce the prohibition of fusion between mother and child, considering that it is prejudicial to the mental health (risk of psychic death and obstacle to the child's normal development) and the integration of the taboo of incest.

When observing the impact of these rites in psychoanalysis, we can refer to the Lacanian theory about the mothering function and its purpose. Indeed, Govindama explains that this function underlines the mother's lacks, thus introducing a symbolic maternal role, and allowing access to the very concept of symbolization through the mother's presence/absence and the exercise of symbolization taking place within the idea of desire as a prelude to the acceptance of the Name-of-the-Father. Therefore, we can imagine that the concept of desire comes from lack because one comes to want what is missing in an attempt to obtain satisfaction. This representation of wholeness is displaced from the mother to the Name-of-the-Father, placing this entity at the higher level of the symbolic hierarchy while giving the subject a rightful place out of the fusion and equidistant to the mother. Moreover, Govindama's analysis of rites for the Goddess Petiaye/Karteri (discussed in Chap. 3) brilliantly metaphorizes the mother's duality and fusional destructive fantasies. These rites allow the parents to project their impulses onto the deity and reaffirm their child's status in the family and society.

In the repetition of these rites throughout life, we can observe the mechanisms and phases cited above and see how they contribute to reaffirming the permanence of the Name-of-the-Father. This entity represents the concept of social authority, at the basis of every relationship; it is the third party to every interaction, presiding over exchanges. Every culture and society has internal mechanisms to manage fear, anxiety, and impulses. The place given to the Name-of-the-Father should always be left vacant, as it must remain a reference or an indication of the permanence of the taboo of incest, maintaining the order of society.

In this chapter, we will describe and analyze the rite of marriage and observe how the concepts Govindama explains are demonstrated. Then we will discuss the idea of giving, drawing from the work of Marcel Mauss, Devereux, Lévi-Strauss, and Lacan. And finally, we will see how adornment plays a specific role as an envelope in the subject's last phase of integration. This will allow us to understand its purpose as a container and vehicle of socialization and a masquerade aiming for social validation while hiding contentious female aspects.

The Senegalese Wolof wedding ritual (Diop, 2011) is conducted by the paternal aunt (*bajjën*). She represents the female version of the patriarchal authority in the family and officiates as such. The ritual consists of a process of bathing and dressing the bride with key instruments while explaining the context of marriage and what is expected from her. It takes place after the civil and religious wedding before she departs to the groom's house. During the previous phase of this ritual, the bride should remain seated on her parent's bed, covered with a veil, more often during the religious wedding. Then, when the wedding is announced, she leaves this position and participates in the ceremony before the ritual bath. This is the last moment she spends as a girl and marks her change of status, to become a wife, a member of the groom's family, and, more specifically, a vessel to carry and pass along their lineage.

During the ritual bath, a calabash is used to carry offerings, the nature of which depends on the specific ethnic group or culture. While the Wolof people put silver pieces of jewelry, a kola nut, salt, plants, and cereal (rice or millet), others (e.g., Fulani people) may add an ox bone.

The remainder of the salt and the calabash are kept for the bride to be used in her household for cooking. This ritual bath is an essential phase of the wedding because it is a necessary step before the bride's departure.

The water symbolizes a death in her lineage, to be reimbursed by offerings. The calabash is somehow a double, an envelope she keeps from her former status, mimicking her initial placenta, and follows her in her new home as a protector or a witness. We can imagine this ritual bath as a requiem of the initial birth and naming ritual, where the individual is affiliated to a lineage and recognizes their human condition. This initial ritual states and underlines the Absent, Great Other, the guarantor of social rules. The paternal aunt commands this ritual as a representative of the Absent. To the bride, she is a mother that echoes the phallic function and shows a good example. In specific contexts, she is called "female-father" (Diop, 1985), underlining her representativeness of the lineage as a woman. This initiation is a repetition that also prepares the bride for her future social role, where she may act as such.

Furthermore, to summarize this ritual, using Van Gennep's definition of its phases, we describe it in the following three steps:

1. The preliminary phase when the bride remains alone in her parent's room, sitting on their bed, symbolizing her origin and departure from the union of a couple and family. This preliminary phase takes place simultaneously with the negotiation and wedding discussions between families. It shows that the bride is taken from a home and should be returned to that home if the marriage is terminated.
2. The second phase is the preliminary experience, where the ritual bath is performed. The *bajjën* advises her niece and explains how this is a new phase of her life. This bath, into which she is plunged, represents the mythical experience, where the water symbolizes the infinity of time and the generations of her lineage.
3. Finally, the third and last phase is when she is dressed in her bridal cloth, provided by the in-laws. She is completely covered in a traditional blanket and leaves her household after receiving her father's blessings. She will only be uncovered upon arrival at the in-laws'. In this last phase, she changes her status and is presented to the in-laws as a wife.

During the three phases of this rite, we can see that clothes are symbols of status; they are envelopes defining borders, from one family to the other and from one generation to the other.

Issa Laye Thiam (2005) has analyzed the initiation ritual of Sereer women in Senegal. According to this author, this ritual is meant to prepare the woman for her role as a future mother and housekeeper, to teach her different ritual techniques, and explain concepts of sexuality. Young women who were to be initiated were gathered and had to take off their clothes at the command of a griot. Thiam describes ritualistic nudity as a return to nature and purity and sees it as a form of sexual education. Nonetheless, here again, we can underline the role of clothes as covers, limits, and status symbols. Without their clothes, young women can express their nature and are invited to expel their impulses through rhythmic dances. In addition, we can see how the body takes place in the ritual, telling the true nature of women, apart from the work of culture and body techniques. This moment shared as a group of initiated is an invitation to arouse desire and sensuality, and these feelings will provide courage and motivation to undergo the pain.

Tattooing (gums and lips) is another aspect of adornment, and Thiam analyzes the procedure for young candidates. Here again, the paternal aunt is the one giving the permission and providing the fees. She will be repaid with a share of her niece's wedding presents. For the tattoo ritual, candidates must be purified, and ask their ancestors' permission. The community attends the ceremony as witness to the candidates' courage. A black cloth is used to cover the candidate, and as we can imagine, the specificity of the cloth and its color is meaningful for the change of status. In fact, the candidate shows her resistance to pain, to become a woman, and after this experience, she is accepted as such.

4.1.2 Giving and Receiving in the Cycle of Exchange

To better explain and analyze the wedding ritual cited above, we will revisit Marcel Mauss's work on the gift, and more specifically the gifts to the ancestors and the process of exchange performed in the wedding ritual. First, we will speak about the gifts exchanged by families, and secondly, about the nature of the gift to the ancestors.

According to Mauss (1950, p. 173),[1] "gifts seal the marriage, form a kinship between the two couples of parents. They give to the two 'sides' the same nature, and this identity of nature is well demonstrated by the prohibition which from now on, will taboo, since the beginning of the engagement, until the end of their days, the two groups of parents who no longer see, or communicate with each other, but exchange perpetual presents. This prohibition expresses both the intimacy and the fear reigning between this kind of creditors and this kind of reciprocal debtors" (1967, p. 13).

In Senegal, after welcoming the bride, the families start a gift exchange ceremony that is highly important for the success of the marriage. There is a code for the amount, nature, and recipients, but the value depends on the families' abilities (Diop, 1985; Thiam, 2005).

The in-laws are supposed to welcome the bride as their own; however, they usually represent a lifelong challenge for her. She stays a stranger, an observer, a witness to their privacy. We may analyze this aspect by referring to Mauss's work on the gift remaining the property of its former owner and representing a threat if not fully repaid. Indeed, her presence in the proximity of their family allows her to witness their flaws, especially when the large family shares a single household. In the everyday language, the bride is "given" by her family to the groom, who "takes" her from her parents. Thus, she is the gift, even if the exchange is reciprocal through her parents' adoption of the groom.

Additionally, she is accountable for the children's fate, which is highly valuable, considering that they belong to the husband's family and will represent their legacy. Simultaneously, the groom's family can observe, analyze, criticize the bride, and extend these critiques to her family. As discussed in the previous chapter, she is more representative of her

[1] Translated from original quote in French: "Les présents scellent le mariage, forment une parenté entre les deux couples de parents. Ils donnent aux deux "côtés" même nature, et cette identité de nature est bien manifestée par l'interdit qui dorénavant, tabouera, depuis le premier engagement de fiançailles, jusqu'à la fin de leurs jours, les deux groupes de parents qui ne se voient plus, ne s'adressent plus la parole, mais échangent de perpétuels cadeaux. En réalité, cet interdit exprime, et l'intimité et la peur qui règnent entre ce genre de créditeurs et ce genre de débiteurs réciproques" (Mauss, 1950, p. 173).

mother's virtue than the groom is of his father's. Therefore, bride and groom are hyphens between the two families and will represent their alliance. Claude Lévi-Strauss (1967) confirms this point, stating that this exchange is only the beginning of an endless process of reciprocal gifts, accomplishing the transition from hostility to an alliance, anxiety to trust, and fear to friendship.[2] The distance created between them and described by Mauss as a taboo between reciprocal debtors aims to avoid any kind of disagreement. Moreover, the marriage system is organized with the inclusion of witnesses embodied by friends and family members to take the lead on any matter, avoiding personal conflicts between the parents. Society will be more likely to impute a marriage's dysfunction to women than men, and all the causal reasoning is organized in this direction.

Devereux, drawing on the ideas of Lévi-Strauss and Marcel Mauss, gives us his approach to the concept of exogamy and the circulation of women. He also questions the role of men in this exchange. In his work, he states that the ritual of marriage does not have the essential goal of creating a bond between husband and wife, or even an alliance between two families. Its function is to mask hostility by proclaiming the creation of a partnership. In other words, it is primarily a transaction between men about women. He adds that the circulation of women and especially their exchange is linked through the law of Talion to an obsessive tendency to what he calls "bilanism" (1965, p. 227), or the compulsive search for symmetry, with all that this kind of obsession entails of latent homosexuality, jealousy, and desire for revenge. Therefore, in Devereux's conception, women are exchanged as gifts between men. These transactions are regulated and contain some specific prohibitions. For societies to give so much importance to their circulation, women must represent the highest currency as a value and a sign.

Furthermore, Lévi-Strauss goes deeper into the idea of women as signs and parts of the language. The primary rules of society have been grounded on the construction of codes to manage them (1967, p. 568).

[2] Translated from original quote in French: "L'échange des fiancés n'est que le terme d'un processus ininterrompu de dons réciproques, qui accomplit le passage de l'hostilité à l'alliance, de l'angoisse à la confiance, de la peur à l'amitié" (Les Structures élémentaires de la parenté, 1967, p. 13).

This leads us to the question of this fear of losing control. Is this evidence of their strength not disguised under the traits of a currency? Indeed, every transaction is operated for the sake and under the supremacy of the Great Other, the Name-of-the-Father, who intervened after the Maternal Other. They all act as a second separation between mother and daughter and underline the latter's belonging to her father's lineage. The *bajjën*'s leadership during the ritual emphasizes this aspect.

So what is being said by the paternal family during this ritual?

- (To the mother): She is ours to give and not yours.
- (To the daughter): You are now offered to your husband's family, and you will provide children for them.

The exchange process is an eternal repetition of transactions connecting people and creating families. Women are at the center of this exchange. Nevertheless, society is conscientious to never let them obtain leadership. Thus, they play their role and, through every exchange, confirm their submission because one important goal of this ritual is to actualize the separation between mother and daughter and prevent a maternal fusion for her future relationship with her children. The layers are always covering their bodies through the rituals, enacting this disguise and symbolizing the Great Other with a highly feminine attribute. Later in this section, we will talk about this attribute and try to analyze its true symbolism.

The second topic we will address in this section is the gifts to the ancestors used in the bath during the wedding ritual. We have defined the actors of the ritual and how the bride is given to her new family. In addition, we have situated the giver, the lineage she comes from, representing the Great Other. When gifts are plunged into the sacred bath, they are offered to her original family to pay her debt of life.

The calabash as the primary accessory for this ritual is another feminine attribute of the Great Other. In our previous work (Diop, 2019), we thoroughly analyzed its feminine symbolism as a double of the placenta, mimicking the creation and assigning the Great Other as the primary carrier. In this ritual, the operation is reproduced, and gifts are offered to replace the girl. The offering of food (cereal and salt) is essential for the ceremony and symbolizes the wishes granted by the ancestors. The family asks for blessings to release the bride and wishes for her to settle in a household where she will always have food for cooking. This point is essential because, culturally, in Senegal, women are solely responsible for the food in the household. This gift of salt aims to wish her master of her home and to keep her marriage in place for long. She will use the rest of the salt in her house, thus prolonging the effect of their blessing.

Mauss has studied the concept of leftovers in sacred gifts, and his findings are relevant to this section. Gifts to the ancestors are essential because when they are not appropriately given, they become a curse. Mauss has worked on the meaning of sacrifices in Hinduism and has seen how the leftovers of the sacrifice are blessed (1950, p. 244). Here, the residual salt protects the bride and grants safe passage from one lineage to the other when added to the bath. The calabash used as a vessel echoes creations at three levels:

- as a carrier for the bride to recall her affiliation to her initial lineage
- as a tool in performing the ritual, acting as a double of the bride in the transaction with the ancestors
- as a protector in her new life, and a remainder of her origin

Thus, in this transaction, the ingredients are compensation for the bride. Silver pieces of jewelry bring supplementary value to the gift when added to the water. This metal is carefully chosen as it traditionally protects from others' malevolence, so all the gifts in the calabash are wishes for the girl who leaves the bath charged with their blessings. The *bajjën* gives what she wishes for her niece's life, and her offerings are also plunged into the bath. The calabash she uses to gather the ingredients is the primary tool for water pouring and cooking later because the bride will use it to rinse her rice in her everyday life.

When analyzing the tattoo ritual cited earlier, we observe the role of pieces of broken clay jars into which the products are poured. In this case, these containers are pieces with a previous history traveling through time and stages of life, accompanying women from one status to the next. These are reserved for her physical appearance and draw a clear connection between their access to womanhood, femininity, and their submission to the Great Other. These pieces, as much as they represent the lineage, are fundamentally connected to land and nature, thus recalling womanhood and mother nature. Hence, the Maternal Other, under this disguise, is also invited to the ritual melted into the figure of the Great Other; however, she is seemingly the witness, and master of the transaction.

This is evidence that women's adornment, at certain stages of life, represents this duality between the Maternal Other and the Great Other. In one dimension, it shows their attractiveness and strong creativity, and in the other dimension, their submission to the order, guarantor of social rules. Rites of passage are the perfect scene to observe these interactions and the position of men and women in this cycle of exchange. Adornment is a set of attributes representing the game of power between these concepts of natural attraction to the Maternal Other and submission to the law of the Great Other. In the next section, we will see how those attributes are chosen, administered, and used.

4.1.3 Costumes and Their Cultural Symbolism

The bride is a gift, and as such, she is hidden and covered with a specific layer. In this section, we will discuss the nature of this cover, its purpose, and its symbolism.

During naming and wedding rituals, a plaid in the woven fabric is used respectively to hold the baby and to cover the bride. This plaid is traditionally woven using a loom. Its color is not relevant, as the family can choose it aesthetically; what matters is that it is a traditional piece. The woven specificity of this accessory reminds us of the idea of generations, and we cannot help but make a link between these rituals and the concept of the superego. Indeed, the perpetuation of rites serves the purpose of transmission, but this cannot happen without transformation, from one generation to the other. According to André Carel (2005), what is transmitted through the law of the Great Other is the superego. This author specializes in family psychoanalysis, and the generational question attracts his attention, in its close relationship with the organization of the family when a child is born.

One's reaction draws its explanation from one's past but also from that of one's ancestors. According to this author, transmission without transformation is a limited concept because each psyche and each interpreting apparatus is singular and specific to a context. Everybody inherits a legacy from his or her ancestors, and upon reception, this psychic material is transformed in a particular way in relation to the context and the related affects.

According to Carel, the superego is "the red thread of generational processes," in reference to Goethe's quote (1809) in *Les Affinités électives*:

> All the ropes of the royal fleet, from the strongest to the weakest, are braided in such a way that a red thread runs through them all and cannot be extracted, without the whole being unraveled, and the smallest fragment still allows one to recognize that they belong to the crown.[3]

Thus, the superego is transmitted from generation to generation, modifying itself by a process of transmission-transformation. The superego perpetuates from the past by transmitting its own form of conflict management, and each generation receives and transmits this legacy to its descendants. This occurs in such a way that even over several generations, the same mode of conflict management is preserved as the sign of recognition for this family, like the rope evoked by Goethe's quote.

Adapting this reasoning to our woven fabric, and underlining the context of the ritual, its purpose to recognize the ancestor's authority, we can imagine that its symbolic value is centered on the reference to the Absent ancestor, guarantor of social patriarchal order, and conveying the representation of the super-ego as an inheritance of the lineage. As the ropes are braided with that red thread, to represent their belonging to the army, the woven plaid is a reference to history and lineage. As much as many of the wedding accessories have been actualized, using new materials, the calabash and the woven plaid have remained traditional. They are symbolic references and retain their value as the red thread, underlining their connection to the lineage, during the rituals, in different stages of life.

[3] "Tous les cordages de la flotte royale, du plus fort au plus faible, sont tressés de telle sorte qu'un fil rouge les parcourt tout entiers et qu'on ne peut l'en extraire, sans que l'ensemble se défasse, et le plus petit fragment permet encore de reconnaître qu'ils appartiennent à la couronne."

Nonetheless, they are a feminine attribute, and the woven plaid is chosen aesthetically and has a prestigious value, in terms of quality and design. They both echo femininity and as such they are also references to the Maternal Other. Therefore, we see here again how both accessories play a double game of representation, supposedly showing submission to the Great Other but implicitly underlining their symbolic reference to the maternal function and thus to the Maternal Other.

Next, let's think about the white color of the bridal cloth offered by the in-laws and worn after the ritual bath. We have discussed in the previous section about the white color, symbol of purity and often used in the context of marriage in different cultures. In this section, we will focus more on this clothing's symbolism than on its color.

The bridal cloth is given to the bride as her first clothing to be worn immediately after the bathing ritual. This represents her new identity and is a costume to remind her of her new status. Earlier, we introduced the Ego-Skin as a concept from Didier Anzieu to explain how primary interactions help to build body image and representations. We have hypothesized that adornment is closely linked to this concept and underlines narcissistic aspects of our personality. In this case, the new clothing is given to demonstrate a change in status, but beyond the simple status, it reflects a modification in the designation. Indeed, the bride as a signifier no longer refers to her family but now belongs to her husband's; therefore, her affiliation has changed, and this is what this clothing represents.

Here, the clothing not being hers or even chosen by her does not allow any narcissistic projection of self-representation, but rather an erasure of such representation, to imprint a new identity, one of purity and newness to welcome the in-laws' codes and rules. Furthermore, she represents a new page where the family's history will continue to be written, up to the next generation. There, they will be able to continue their process of transmission-transformation and convey their ancestors' heritage.

Thus, adornment is used here to show or declare a status, but the message it sends is not that of self-representation because since it is given by the in-laws, they are the narrators and storytellers deciding which role the bride will play in this story. Nevertheless, adornment may be a form of expression for the Ego-Skin and serve a narcissistic purpose at a personal level when it is chosen, but represents the submission to codes of society and/or lineage when it is imposed. In the next chapter, we will see how clothing can be a way for women to grasp their own image and choose their value as a sign.

Returning to the Sereer tattoo ritual, let's focus on the use of clothing during the different phases of the ritual. In the first phase, where candidates are naked, the absence of clothes has a meaning. They are undressed to return to their nature, where no status or codes apply. This rhythmic dance allows complete detachment of rules, and frees the body, letting the "feminine jouissance" burst out, revealing the reference to the Maternal Other. She gathers strength and courage from the dance, in her primary nature, her femininity. However, the tattoo ceremony being under the auspices of the Great Other testifies its supremacy, on the candidate's body, status, and destiny. The black cloth covering the candidate during the ritual seems to be a reference to her lineage, here again echoing the idea of transmission and history.

In this section, we have seen how rituals give meaning to adornment, and show through symbolic references the connections between the Great Other, reference of the ancestor, and the Maternal Other, primary all-powerful phallic figure. They take part in the rituals, sometimes alternatively and sometimes conjointly, through specific symbols of adornment, marking their territory on the female body. The process of transmission-transformation conveys the ancestors' heritage, and simultaneously makes a reference to the Maternal Other, signifying her implicit participation in the rituals.

Women are tied in the exchange cycle; they are given as wives, and then provide children. During the different phases of their lives, punctuated by rites of passage, they are reminded that they belong to an order, and that they do not own their children. It seems that all these rituals have in common the purpose to avoid the installation of a fantasy of omnipotence, or the exaggeration of the maternal function: to completely absorb her child as her own gift. Indeed, the maternal fusion, in the first place, equals the termination of everything: language, culture, and society.

In the next section, we will introduce social representations of status through adornment. We will see how society has historically used clothing, hairdressing, and jewelry to reflect social roles and hierarchy.

4.2 External Signs of Social Classes

4.2.1 Gold as a Privilege for the Higher Classes

Historians stressed the importance of jewelry in West Africa. As far as they were able to reconstitute the past, they found that adornment was essential in defining people's identity, gender, and social class. Davidson (1967, p. 52), in his work on African kingdoms, has described ancient paintings, found in the region of the Tassili (North Africa). Paradoxically to the classic description of North African women, as less involved in work and chores (farming, herding, raising children, sewing clothes, making pottery, basketry, and cooking), the author underlines their active representation in art. For the two paintings he describes, a lot of attention was given to details like women's skin color carnation, their sophisticated outfits, accessories, and hairstyles. Davidson interprets this as a certain respect given to women at this moment in history.

Majhemout Diop (1972, p. 39–44) has conducted research on the history of social classes in West Africa. He studied the status of nobility in ancient Senegal and presented higher classes' hereditary privileges. According to him, noble women and their ladies had every right on judiciary, social, and feminine matters. This status was particularly underlined by their exclusive right to wear golden jewelry. These accessories, in addition to their clothing, dance, manners, and language, distinguish them from others. In fact, many historians or tale writers have described prestigious feminine figures, paying a lot of attention to their fine gestures, expensive jewelry, and delicate clothing. This representation is confirmed in travel journals, bringing an immersive approach to society from travelers' perspectives.

Feminine adornment includes hairstyle, which can differ from one family to the other, determining social class and ranking. Bernolles (1966, p. 13) observed how hairstyles were reproduced and accessorized in diverse parts of sub-Saharan Africa. He interprets this as a result of the migration and dissemination of one specific population: Fulbés. However, from a research point of view, we would instead consider this as trends exchanged and communicated from certain countries and places to others. Perhaps because Bernolles imagined Africa as ancient and not as evolutive as other places, he underestimated the possible connections and communication channels already in place at this moment in history, which could have promoted these adornment styles and reinforced their dissemination.

Noirot's travel journal is a rich piece. The author collected anecdotes and fine details of his travels through Fouta Djallon (located in Guinea Conakry) and Bambouc (now in southeast Senegal and West Mali). During his stay, he described women's aesthetics, clothing, and pieces of jewelry.

In his observation of the Fulani people, he describes his host's wives' adornment, and we can see how their role and ranking are displayed:

> They are neither beautiful nor ugly; they are neatly dressed in a local loin-cloth and wear jewels on their head, neck, arms, and legs. The husband introduces them to us according to their rank in his affection.
>
> (…) Fatimata is the queen of the house; she does not lack jewels; six silver five-franc coins hanging from the braids of her hair, on both sides of her face; a necklace of large amber balls surrounds her neck; large silver bracelets adorn her wrists and ankles. She wears all this glitter with distinction.
>
> Successively, Mariama (Marie) Aïsatou, Iaé (Jeanne) and Fatou are presented to us. Younger, they have less jewelry than the first. Fatou, who humbly stands aside, has only her beauty and sad smile for adornment. Captive of origin…[4]

---

[4]Translated from original quote in French: "Elles ne sont ni belles ni laides; très proprement vêtues d'un pagne du pays, elles portent des bijoux à la tête, au cou, aux bras et aux jambes. Le mari nous les présente par ordre, selon le rang qu'elles occupent dans son affection.

(…) Fatimata est la reine du logis; les bijoux ne lui font pas défaut; six pièces de cinq francs en argent accrochés aux nattes de sa chevelure, pendent de chaque côté du visage; un collier de grosses boules d'ambre entoure son cou; de gros bracelets d'argent ornent ses poignets et ses chevilles. Elle porte tout ce clinquant avec distinction.

Successivement mesdames Mariama (Marie) Aïsatou, Iaé (Jeanne) et Fatou nous sont présentées. Moins anciennes, elles ont moins de bijoux que la première. Fatou qui humblement se tient à l'écart, n'a pour parure que sa beauté et son sourire triste. Captive d'origine…" (Noirot, 1881, p. 86–87).

Here we can see how the first wife's adornment underlines her nobility and distinguishes her from the others. As the first, she commands the household and receives her co-wives' respect and submission. The last wife, Fatou, in contrast, is not wearing any jewelry, and her status as a captive, of an inferior class, confirms this ranking. This also supports Mahjemout Diop's analysis and shows that this rule in Senegal is shared in the Fouta Djallon.

Additionally, hairstyling using jewels seems to be another way to enhance beauty and show prestige. Hairstyles are sophisticated, and their construction can take up to two days (Noirot, 1881, p. 223). We can imagine that people in the highest classes were more likely to have the more sophisticated hairstyles, considering that they would have more resources, in terms of people, time, money, and accessories.

In his travel journal, Mungo Park (1795) was also interested in hairstyling in the region of The Gambia. He identified a specifically feminine hairstyle using a cotton headscarf, pieces of white glass, and a small piece of gold worn on the forehead. This hairstyle seemed to be quite prestigious and was reserved for specific classes. In another region of West Africa, the same author reports other types of hairdressing using accessories like seashells and textiles.

We have seen how gold is a representation of high status; it signifies not only the woman's rank but also her husband's or father's wealth, showing the powerful house they inhabit or come from. Giving access to golden pieces of jewelry to wives or daughters is a way to resonate in the eye of the viewer, for the husband and the father. In addition, for wives and daughters, wearing golden pieces of jewelry is a way to show higher standards than others (women or men).

Tierno Monénembo, in his novel Le Roi de Kahel, a fiction based on history (2008), describes a princess in the Fouta Djallon and insists on her varied choice of jewelry, golden and precious pearls, necklaces, pieces of gold in her braids, and so on. This transcribes her wealth and power in the region when the author notes that she is even wealthier than her husband, the prince. This wealth makes her even more powerful and allows her to have a status of freedom, making her independent, seductive, and belligerent.

Therefore, pieces of jewelry used as adornment have the effect of impressing others and showing power. As such, they can be narcissizing for the person who wears them and comfort them in a position of superiority compared to those who do not. Thus, we can understand the rule forbidding lower classes to wear gold because it would terminate this superiority of nobility over the rest of society.

Boubacar Barry (1972) studied the history of the Waalo and described how society was structured and organized. As in many places, nobility was not earned but transmitted from one generation to the next. People in this position had privileges and natural superiority over their slaves, whom they inherited from their parents. In their place, they also had duties to their people and had to give (food, shelter, protection, etc.) in return.

Thus, adornment is another way in which society maintains a specific rule. Nonetheless, the limitations women could face regarding their adornment are notable, especially when their hairstyling was representative of their family totem. In this case, we can imagine that adornment was not prestigious or personal and was merely a way to confirm the individual's belonging to their lineage.

In the next section, we will see how clothing was described, manufactured, and developed in the past in the West African region. Again, we will use travel journals as references for the most precise descriptions.

4.2.2 Society Structured by Adornment

Travel journals (Park, 1795; Caillie, 1824–1828; Noirot, 1881) also bring extensive information about people's clothing. In the Fouta Djallon, Noirot describes it as simple for both men and women. According to him, at this moment in history, women's clothes were even more basic than men's, consisting of a piece of cloth tied at the hip. Like men, women had amulets enclosed in leather bags. They also wore silver coins tied in necklaces, as well as balls of amber, coral, or glass beads in the braids of their hair.

Men are responsible for making and sewing clothes, and boys were dressed as soon as they were eleven and girls as soon as they were nine. Regarding the fabric, women were experts at dyeing, using natural indigo coloring extract.

Mungo Park's observation of Mandingo clothing, gathered during his travels, reveals a different dress code for women:

> The women's clothing consists of two pieces of cloth, six feet long and three feet wide; one girdled around their loins, and falling to the ankle, has the effect of a skirt; the other casually wrap their breast and shoulders[5] (Park, 1795, p. 49–50).

In his travel journals, Rene Caillie (1824–1828) also extensively described West African people. Thus, we can note that in this part of West Africa, there is a difference in clothing for women depending on ethnic group. Mandingo women used to hide the upper part of their body, whereas Fulani women living in the Fouta Djallon did not.

We have seen how society was structured into classes and how gold represented some privilege for higher ranks. We note that for people in various parts of West Africa, the principal difference in adornment was through the preciousness of material for jewelry and beads. Indeed, the variety of materials (coral, seashells, gold stones, etc.) offered women many options for adornment. However, gold seemed to be reserved for the higher classes in every part of West Africa, representing their superiority over people from the lower classes. Another difference appears for enslaved people, who also showed a difference in clothing because they could only obtain them from their masters. The wealthier and nobler you were, the more likely you were to have access to clothes and accessories. This rule did not seem to be limited to this period or this region but rather universal.

Children are kept naked until a certain age; as mentioned earlier, this gives an impression of equality among them. Thus, the affirmation of classes only starts when children attain puberty, and are hence closer to the age of marriage. Therefore, it is only when the process of exchange starts that each member of society, depending on their class, elevates their status or increases the appearance of their nobility with jewelry and

[5]Translated from original quote in French: "L'habillement des femmes consiste en deux pièces de toile, de six pieds de long et de trois pieds de larges; l'une ceinte autour de leurs reins, et tombant jusqu'à la cheville du pied, fait l'effet d'une jupe; l'autre enveloppe négligemment leur sein et leurs épaules."

hairstyling. This process is connected to the full exchange, as Mauss defines it, since society promotes unions and alliances and defines rules of clothing, jewelry wearing, and hairstyling for everybody, depending on their status. Nevertheless, the artistry, grace, and taste are singular to each and reveal their resonance. In this particular window, women express their inner capacity to appeal to and capture the gaze of the Other. They gain narcissism through this capacity and use it as an asset for exchange.

These accessories enhance the display of power and arouse attraction. The connection between these factors is evident. On the one hand, women use ways to show their potential, by means of accessories and body techniques. On the other hand, their identity, lineage, and status are assets to show social power over others. Their attractiveness represents not only their inner value but also that of their family and their strength in the social arena. Mauss described the total exchange between people as a way to demonstrate their collective power, showing their jewels and most precious accessories. Adornment in West African celebrations, especially in the exchange of gifts in ritualistic ceremonies, represents the full exchange. The better the accessories, the more potent and valuable their carrier. In this perspective, women use accessories to reflect their nobility and inner worth. They thus appear more substantial in the eyes of the Other.

4.2.3 Gold in African Cultures

We have seen how adornment is used to represent wealth and prestige. Jewels are practical tools of social recognition. Gold was historically chosen as the most precious metal, and the variety of jewelry testifies to this. Earlier, we have shown how higher classes were keen to wear golden jewels, the prestige of their status. Kings and chiefs wore various golden accessories such as scepters, ornaments, bracelets, crowns, hair plates, and necklaces.

Garrard (1989) makes an inventory of all golden accessories in West Africa, presenting goldwork from Ghana, Ivory Coast, Mali, and Senegal. According to him, this region was very creative in this field because not only did they retain their originality, but they also incorporated foreign influences, creating an infinite variety of designs. Goldsmiths were not only working in gold but also silver, swords, chains, and copper; therefore, they had a central place in society. Indeed, the system of castes, including that of the smiths, remains profoundly anchored in West Africa.

The same author remarks that West African jewelry was not widely represented in museums or private collections within or outside of Africa despite its wealth. Because of its symbolism in the family history, royal and noble families often keep it as an heirloom, passing it from one generation to the next. Moreover, gold is usually recycled and melted into new designs, diminishing the number of ancient and traditional models.

As a symbol of power, gold was also targeted in times of war. Kings' golden regalia and their royal accessories were usually ransacked during conflicts. Indeed, Gallard takes as an example the Asante king who suffered a disastrous defeat at the battle of Katamanso in 1826 and lost not only his wives and daughters but also his royal badges, golden weapons, jewels, scepters, and umbrellas (1989, p. 15). The enemy took ownership of all his victims' goods and privileges. In this example, women symbolize the king's high status, as do his golden accessories. The enemy takes possession of them as he does the power.

Another passage of Gallard's writing shows how golden accessories were essential to the king's demonstration of power; he quotes North African visitors describing a king from the Ghanaian empire:

The king adorns himself like a woman wearing necklaces round his neck and bracelets on his forearms, and he puts on a high cap decorated with gold and wrapped in a turban of file cotton. He sits in audience… in a doomed pavilion around embroidered cloth. Behind the king stand ten pages holding shields and swords decorated with gold, and on his right are the sons of the vassal kings of his country… their hair plaited with gold… At the door of the pavilion are dogs of excellent pedigree who hardly ever leave the place where the king is, guarding him. Round their necks, they wear collars of gold and silver studded with a number of balls of the same metals. (1989, p. 30)

The king possessed such a large number of jewels and golden accessories because he represents the highest nobility and power. This confirms the idea of jewelry symbolizing prestige and nobility reserved for the highest classes. The king's pages and dogs are also accessories and decorations, representing his power.

In folkloric literature, as Amadou Hampathé Ba writes, the witch is mighty in the tale of Ndjeddo Dewal, and her seven daughters wear many golden accessories. They are emblems of their mother's wealth. Moreover, Mamy Wata wears many jewels, representing her magic power and the opportunity to become wealthier with her help.

Indeed, the literature representing figures of power emphasizes their rich adornment, especially when they are women. Gold not only represents royalty but also wealth and power, that of persuasion and illusion.

In his description of the princess of Fouta Djallon, Monènembo emphasizes her cleverness and beauty. Her many jewels and accessories demonstrate her wealth; she is not only the prince's wife but is herself a lord and landowner. These accessories and her power make her more substantial than the noblest man.

In sum, kings adorn themselves like women to show their power, and women who adorn themselves like kings have more power. Thus, it seems that the signs being communicated here are not genders (men or women) but power and adornment. This is where the actual exchange lies.

To conclude this chapter, we can state that adornment sends a message to subjects themselves, and then to society. On the one hand, it locates the first in their lineage, referring to the ancestors and declaring their affiliation. And on the other hand, it places them in a social position toward other members of society. In this intersection between the subject and their community, adornment comprises a set of tools for self-expression and valorization. It allows narcissization and, through thin interstices, allows the subject to communicate their identity. The Ego-Skin transpires in that intersection, plugging pieces of aesthetics together to fill in the lack. Women, through their aesthetic attributes, imprint their personal history and problematics and communicate their value as signs. While their aesthetic appears to cover their nudity, it can paradoxically underline their strength. The ritualistic nudity used in the tattoo ceremony has shown how clothing has the role of taming impulses. Therefore, we can imagine how adornment contains femininity, as much as it reveals it.

In the next chapter, we will discuss the evolution of adornment in West Africa and observe how society and colonization have had an influence on beauty criteria. This will allow us to analyze the mechanism women have built to reveal themselves and navigate into social representations, to design and promote their aesthetic image.

References

Barry, B. (1972). *Le royaume du Waalo le Sénégal avant la conquête.* textes à l'appui François Maspero.
Bernolles, J. (1966). *Permanence de la parure et du masque africains.* Université de Dakar, Faculté des Lettres et Sciences Humaines.
Caillie, R. (1824–1828). *Journal d'un voyage à Timbouctou et à Jenné dans l'Afrique centrale,* Volumes I, II and III, éditions Anthropos Paris.
Carel, A. (2005). L'après-coup générationnel in *Le Générationnel,* coll. Inconscient et Culture, Approche en thérapie familiale psychanalytique, dirigée Par A. Eiguer.
Davidson, B. (1967). *Les royaumes africains,* Collections Time-Life.
Devereux, G. (1965). *Ethnopsychanalyse complémentariste,* chap. 4 : La Notion de Parenté, Flammarion.
Diop, A.-B. (1985). *La famille Wolof, traditions et changements.* Karthala.
Diop, I. (2011). 1. Le Sénégal. In Y. Govindama (Ed.), *Temps et rites de passage: Naissance, enfance, culture et religion* (pp. 21–39). Editions Karthala.
Diop, M. (1972). *Histoire des classes sociales en Afrique de l'Ouest.* François Maspero Paris.
Garrard, T. F. (1989). *Gold of Africa, Jewellery and ornaments from Ghana, Côte d'Ivoire, Mali and Senegal in the collection of the Barbier-Mueller Museum.* Prestel.
Goethe. (1809). *Les Affinités électives.*
Govindama, Y. (2006). *Le monde hindou à la Réunion, Une approche anthropologique et psychanalytique.* Karthala.
Govindama, Y. (2011). *Temps et rites de passage.* Introduction (pp. 9–19). Karthala.
Lévi-Strauss, C. (1967). *Les structures élémentaires de la parenté.* Mouton & Co and Maison des Sciences de l'Homme.
Mauss, M. (1950). Essai sur le don, forme et raison de l'échange dans les sociétés archaïques. In *Sociologie et Anthropologie.* Presses Universitaires de France.
Monénembo, T. (2008). *Le roi de Kahel.* Éditions du Seuil.
Park, M. (1795). *Voyage dans l'intérieur de l'Afrique,* FM / La Découverte, 1980.
Thiaw, I. L. (2005). *La femme Seereer.* L'Harmattan.

5

Adornment and Social Representation

Social representations have an impact on one's construction of self-image. Women are exposed to social representation at every level of their being: integrity, sexuality, fitness as a spouse or a mother, and professional/intellectual capability. This makes them victims of several stereotypes. Researchers in the United States have identified them to better understand the clinical interaction. Although African women might be exposed to different stereotypes and cultural representations than black women from the United States, we do observe in the clinical interaction that as black women, the consequences of colonization expose them to specific stereotypes.

Regarding social representations of black women persistent in the collective imaginary, bell hooks distinguished four stereotypes (Carberry & Brooks-Gordon, 2020):

1. The masculinization of the black woman: this stereotype is one of the foundations of the myth of 'strong black woman' and paints a black woman who is bearable, tireless, deeply attentive and apparently invulnerable whose function is to take on burdens and complete difficult tasks.

I. S. Diop, *Adornment, Masquerade and African Femininity*, Pan-African Psychologies,
https://doi.org/10.1007/978-3-031-28748-0_5

2. The submissive black woman and the concept of 'sexual savage': this stereotype takes its origin in a patriarchal ideology, misogynist religious teachings and a deep hatred of white slavers originally oriented towards women in general then specifically to black women seen as the embodiment of female evil and lust, as a result of a projection of their own sexual impulses.
3. The nursing woman used for reproduction: during slavery, the main source of profit depended on the number of slaves, so slavers set up a system of forced reproduction based on the threat of beatings. Some women were forced to breastfeed their owner's children at the expense of their own.
4. The concept of authoritarian black women based on the idea that enslaved women adopted and imitated the dominant roles that white women had in their homes. Today, we also talk about the concept of 'black angry woman' (Lee, 2005).

Those stereotypes are not only based on black women's gender and race, but also on the conjunction between both, as well as additional factors such as education and social situation. The concept of Intersectionality refers to the convergence and interactions of the multiple dimensions making cultural identity, which, in turn, has an effect on an individual's personality and perspective (Crenshaw, 1989; Jordan-Zachery, 2007; McCall, 2005 as cited in Multicultural Issues in Counseling, p. 24).

Lugones's analysis (2011) of intersectionality revealed that the term "'black woman' is grossly inadequate because racial formation and gender formation are inseparable processes (…) 'man' and 'woman' cannot be reduced to the reproductive; the reproductive itself cannot be thought apart from the racialization of procreation."

She also explains that black women's images were constructed after a long process of subjectivation in response to an internalization of Western-centered normative constructs grounded in denigration and dehumanization. These normative constructs have forced non-white women to build themselves at the margin and through two imposing archetypes: the "white" woman and the black "man." This construction in the invisible did not allow black women to build a racialized and gendered self, a modern rational self. Thus, this erased their resistant subjectivities and the multiplicity of their existences. In fact, a fragmented sense of self has settled in. The negation of the construction of black women created this distorted perspective of non-white women as fictional inferiors. Fictional but real, however, because by denying this intersectional "race-gender," they have made it impossible especially for black women to exercise power and authority, to decolonize their identities and fulfill their rights as proper members of societies.

As a clinical psychologist, the concept of Intersectionality helps the author to apprehend the reality of black female patients, to understand how patients symbolize these identities. Regarding African women, these identities are also connected to social representations and stereotypes attributed to women in their cultures and installed with colonization. This concept also has implications in the transference and countertransference dynamic, because of the perspectives and past experiences of both patient and therapist, depending on where they stand on the spectrum of social classes and cultural backgrounds.

Feminist activists like Nassira Hedjerassi (as cited in bell hooks (1984 and 2000)) have pointed out the inadequacies of this Western-centered feminism and of its "miserabilist, racist views on women from African countries and the Arab world." One of the points highlighted is the "arbitrary character of universalism, not articulated in the experiences of these women." There is an additional question by C. Diop (2013a) who calls to "get out of the dilemma between scientific objectivity and non-objective subjectivity." Diop explains how "the institutional framework of the French social sciences encourages the researchers to claim objectivity stemming from an overhanging position in relation to his research object" (Diop, 2013a).

From African feminists' perspective, the call (Kessi & Boonzaier, 2018) is for the decolonization of knowledge in psychology, to fight against stereotypes reinforcing racist ideologies (Nicholas & Cooper, 1990; El Saadawi, 1997; Mama, 1995; Shervington, 1994; Kanazawa, 2006, Dogra, 2012), epistemic violence (Spivak, 1988), and widespread beliefs in the inferiority of colonized populations (Biko, 1978; Fanon, 1986).

In this chapter, our goal is to describe the evolution of the feminine ideal, through sociocultural representation based on African cultures and influenced by colonization. In the first part, we will discuss the concepts of Blackness and Colorism to understand how women's image was built as a social construct, mirroring society's fears. Then in the second part of this chapter, we will introduce coping strategies and perspectives that women have used to grasp their image and detach from standards and stereotypes. We will use the example of the natural hair movement in this regard. Additionally, we will see how the spiritual field can be used as a transitional space to develop one's identity and gain confidence. We will discuss the role of adornment in these examples and see its relationship with the identity and the Ego-Skin concept.

5.1 Intersectionality and Black Femininity

5.1.1 Blackness and Colonialism

Franz Fanon (1952) has conceptualized the relationship that black men and women have with their white counterparts. He has tried to comprehend how black women understand their relationship with whiteness, through Mayotte Capecia's novel *Black Skin, White Masks.* He vividly criticizes her representation of social ascension associated with her union with a white man. Indeed, this could be seen as a provocative position, because her representation of social ascension perpetuates the glorification of whiteness and despises black men. Nevertheless, Fanon is in a masculine position himself, and does not seem to understand this position as an outcome of several experiences and stereotypes that women in their geographical, social, and personal situations are going through.

According to Fanon, this novel "promotes an unhealthy behavior" (1952, p. 40). What does this mean if not that there is a specific behavior expected from women?

Lewis Gordon (2015) in his research has added a nuance to Fanon's ideas. Indeed, he found that Capecia's history was distorted and modified by white male writers to enhance this image of a submissive black woman dismissing black men. He extends his interpretation to review Fanon's ideas on Lacanian psychoanalytical theories, as they do not take into consideration social information such as race and discrimination to understand people's lived experiences. Thus, what Fanon criticizes about Capecia's position is not really her ideas as a black woman, but white writers' views on the latter.

In the process of defining their identities, women must sometimes fight these stereotypes, and claim their status in society, because the construction of the social territory does not include them in every space, position, or status. Socially and culturally, they are contained in the private space, out of the decision-making process. Moreover, the heroine of this novel sees the union with a white man as a way off of her island, an escape route from the destiny to which women are condemned in her family.

The history of colonialism and the erection of whiteness as a social ideal have shaped and oriented the global definition of beauty. Colonized people have implicitly accepted that they must evolve toward whiteness, physically and mentally, to reach a higher social recognition. For women, this ideology has implied the construction of a vision of womanhood closer to the stereotype of the European woman. The way women talk, think, walk, dress, and take care of themselves is assessed and criticized by society. They are not only judged on their integrity but also compared to this stereotype of European women, because colonization has put the white woman's model at one pole of the woman spectrum, and the black women at its opposite.

In the context of Mayotte Capecia's novel, because of the damages that slavery has created, skin whitening was a survival strategy for a life-threatening situation. Union with a white man is the best way to evolve to have lighter-skinned children and have access to better resources. Whereas, in the context of poverty, and with social inequity, women have less access to professional positions allowing them to earn higher incomes, and the evolution toward the white woman's model (emancipated, free, detached from the model of the benevolent mother) is a viable strategy. Therefore, the white woman's model seems to be close to that of the devouring mother. We have seen previously how African societies have promoted the benevolent mothers, as culturally representative of morals and virtues. In many contexts, women's behaviors are seen as a sign of cultural transmission, as if they are evidence that education and ideology of women's submission are the best ways to maintain social cohesion.

Paradoxically, black men are the ones promoting this white woman stereotype by defining lighter women as representative of their aesthetic ideal. Moreover, it seems like they determine the woman evaluation spectrum, because in the end, women are the object of their desire. How do they come to this phantasm and aesthetic ideal?

Fanon has developed an analysis on this topic, through the stories of two literary characters of black men, one who is attracted to a white woman, in René Maran's novel *Un homme pareil aux autres* (1947), and the other who is attracted to a mixed-race woman in Abdoulaye Sadji's novel *Nini* (1947). In his reflection, he tries to understand how educated black men feel about white women. He describes this feeling as the result of their own social representation in the white world. Because of their education, people no longer consider them as blacks, and their status is dissociated from that of savage blackness. Therefore, they are transported to an in-between where they are no longer black, and not white. In reaction to what the author calls ostracism, they develop a hunger for a relation with white women because only the latter's consideration can validate an advantageous social status.

Thus, beauty criteria were influenced by this situation, and have evolved toward a preference for women who look more like the European model, and hence black men are more likely to choose black women with lighter skin tone, or European hair. We can assume here that whiteness confers social power, and that such a concept originated from colonization, which positioned the white man at the top of the social hierarchy, and the white woman by his side.

Historically, agents working in the colonies had black women as privileges, for their personal satisfaction, and this confirms women's position as objects coming with land ownership. For most of these women, although this situation provided them access to better resources, it was imposed on them. Nowadays, in the context of poverty, the union with foreigners with financial stability can be seen as a way out of the country, and an opportunity for migration, not only for the black woman but also for her family, and thus they are likely to encourage her in this direction. This outcome was what Mayotte Capecia was aiming for, and she could not imagine obtaining what she wanted by herself, on her island, without this man's contribution. In fact, because he was white, a relationship with him made her what she wanted to become.

When Fanon criticizes Mayotte's glorification of whiteness, and willingness to accept anything from her lover, just because he is white, he seems to be referring to the idea of blackness as inferior, and the acceptance of such a paradigm. On that point he is right, because the reader might be drawn to accept this complex of inferiority. However, this does not change the fact that, as the concept of intersectionality addresses, because of their position, women also suffer from this complex of inferiority with men in general. Therefore, black women suffer from stereotypes from all men, regardless of their ethnicity: whether the evaluator is a white man or woman, or a black man, they are always confronted with this spectrum. Black women's representation in the economic world of advertisement and marketing echoes this perspective, as their visibility is recent and still in progress. In fact, their participation in fashion modeling campaigns was still singular in the last twenty years, with only few black icons, compared to the large number of famous white models. Indeed, even in this process, beauty standards are still pointing to the European woman as the positive extreme of the beauty spectrum.

Roberto Beneduce (2006) has written on the topic of Franz Fanon's contribution to critical ethnopsychiatry. He cites Mannoni to address the gap between Europeans and educated people from colonized countries: "Subjects who have evolved according to the Western model become dangerous and their cultural difference is made imperceptible, because it is hidden behind a familiar appearance. It is disturbing: they have studied too much, they are too similar to us, they are more dangerous, they are rebellious"[1] (p. 89).

Thus, we understand how it can be difficult for people at the highest point of their own representation of the social hierarchy to see their supposed superiority challenged. If race is the reason for superiority, then educated people from racialized backgrounds disrupt the usual order. In

[1] "Les sujets qui ont évolué selon le modèle occidental deviennent dangereux et leur différence culturelle est rendue imperceptible, car elle est cachée sous une apparence familière. C'est dérangeant: ils ont trop étudié, ils nous ressemblent trop, ils sont plus dangereux, ils sont rebelles."

the same way, if gender is a reason for superiority, then emancipated women must be equally disturbing.

Education, rites of passage and body techniques have the goal to pass on cultural values and ensure repetition and continuity in lineages. Societies are evolving toward a more equal world, where women have better access to resources; however, stereotypes still reduce their opportunities. To end this perception of the European beauty model as the ideal, and for black women to be accepted within their own beauty parameters, societies must solve this complex of inferiority once and for all.

Hanétha Véthé-Congolo (2020) has revisited the work of Fanon and compared his thinking to Suzanne Césaire's. Indeed, in the latter's work, she presents Mayotte's Capecia's desire for her fight as driven by a need for social progression, imitating the frame and system of a group seen as dominant. Thus, according to this last author, what is represented in this story is not only a romance with a white man, but also all the challenges black women face in their society and their limited options. This fight for social progress is annihilating and leaves the subject with only limited opportunities. The circumstances in which the heroine was raised and her representation of herself is the explanation for this perception of whiteness as superior and perfect.

Developing strategies to accept ourselves depends on the resources we have and social representations we were taught about ourselves and others. If, like Mayotte, women are raised in an environment where options for survival and emancipation are outside of the country, through the relationship with a man, and since only white men can provide social recognition, then it is no wonder that they work toward that goal.

To end this section what we would like to address is the idea that women's bodies are at the center of society's scope: their hairstyles, skin color, personalities, and sexuality are scrutinized. Moreover, these aspects are used to define, criticize, or judge them, and calculate the morals of an entire social group. They are determined as vectors of transmission, but their contribution to social evolution is still controversial or at least controlled. The representation of black femininity as an ideal is a fight that women cannot carry out on their own. They must respond to social realities that came with historical contexts and are still prevalent today.

Hanétha Véthé-Congo has designed the concept of "femmism" to describe mechanisms at work for women of color to overcome those multiple social challenges:

> The term 'femmism' refers to an idea that responds to the crucial question of how one 'femmises' oneself, that is, how by one's actions, thoughts and discourse, the woman maintains herself as such, in a context where she knows she is de facto a woman but where the dominant system in which she evolves and which pretends to structure her absolutely does not recognize her reality as a human being, and consequently her integrity as a subject (woman), and this, strictly by virtue of what the same system qualifies as race.
>
> In sum, 'femmism' translates the capacity and the manner in which the woman has to establish an ethic of transcendence and to act according to it in order to transcend the multiple traumas inflicted upon her as a female subject strictly on the basis of the a-ethical notion of 'race.'[2] (2020, p. 16)

Thus, according to this author, and for Afro-descendant women, "femmism" refers to strategies of adaptation to and confrontation with their reality and challenges. This concept differs from feminism, which carries the idea of the fight for women's emancipation, in that it includes the existential realities of women, without any prejudice regarding what they should or should not stand for. In this perspective, adornment embodies these strategies, as it defines women's appearance and conditions their image and representation in society.

---

[2] Translated from original quote in French: "Le terme 'femmisme' renvoie à une idée répondant à la cruciale question de savoir comment l'on se 'femmise', c'est à dire comment par ses actes, ses pensées et son discours, la femme se maintient femme, dans un contexte où elle se sait de facto femme mais où le système dominant dans lequel elle évolue et qui prétend la structurer ne reconnait absolument pas sa réalité en tant qu'humaine et conséquemment son intégrité en tant que sujet (femme) et ce strictement en vertu de ce que le même système qualifie de race.

En somme le 'femmisme' traduit la capacité et la manière que la femme a d'établir une éthique de la transcendance et d'agir en fonction de celle-ci pour transcender les traumatismes multiples lui étant infligés en tant que sujet femme à proprement parler sur la base de la notion a-éthique de 'race'" (Véthé-Congolo, 2020, p. 16).

5.1.2 Skin Color, Hairstyle, and Identity

Sabine Belliard (2012) has written on the topic of skin color and its impact on identity. She confirms that history has created this representation of racial hierarchy, which has had an effect within the racialized population and generated depreciative representations of dark skin color and kinky hair, against positive representations of light skin color and non-kinky hair. As Belliard notes, this context has shaped the signification of terms used in the common vocabulary. Indeed, words like beautiful, pretty, and elegant are charged with a physical representation, influenced by this racial hierarchy. This has determined how one should look to seduce or get others' attention.

According to Belliard, and in reference to Anzieu's work on the Ego-Skin, "the face presents itself to the other as a screen in his or her internal world; emotional movements are to some extent readable on a face" (2012, p. 66).[3]

When she analyzes her black patients' concerns about their skin color, Belliard notes that it is a sensitive point, about which they feel vulnerable. An insult related to skin color is experienced like an attack on the deepest foundations of their personality, narcissistically devaluating enough to deconstruct their self-esteem. As such, it is the result of people projecting their fears and flaws, through the topic of skin color.

In recent years, many campaigns have had the goal to valorize black skin and break stigmas. Some countries have even banned skin bleaching products and taken legal action against distributors. However, personalities and celebrities using these kinds of products and thus promoting this lifestyle contribute to maintaining stereotypes depreciating dark skin color. Skin bleaching products are available for every budget, and some chemical formulas have proven invasive and even dangerous for their users. When thinking of the skin as a screen showing one's internal world, and taking the example of skin lightening, we can imagine that people feel the need to adorn their skin, to feel narcissistically valorized by the

[3]Translated from original quote in French: "Le visage se présente à l'autre comme un écran dans son monde interne; les mouvements émotionnels sont dans une certaine mesure, lisibles sur un visage."

other. Thus, their regular appearance, being charged with depreciative representations, affects the way they feel in others' eyes, and creates a breach making them vulnerable. In this case, the adornment, through skin-lightening, has the ability to close that breach and change the skin, and with it our identity.

Returning to the concept of Ego-Skin, the fact that the skin barrier is the first point of contact with the other, the limit of our envelope, marking boundaries of our self, and analyzing it through the social representation of races and the beauty spectrum, we can imagine how symbolic the skin is to someone, in their appearance. Skin color is one of the most memorable descriptive attributes, and its appreciation precedes that of one's identity. Skin bleaching introduces a new variable, as people can choose their skin color, and navigate in nuances at will. In this perspective, we can say that to some extent, using such products is taking a position to change ourselves and modify our initial envelope. However, women being primary clients, because they are more often expected to comply with beauty ideals, diminishes the idea of independence attached to the concept of choice.

How does one come to have the will to change one's body to appear socially valued? This question takes us back to the representation of women in society. They impersonate men's desires and adorn themselves in the direction of social beauty criteria. Thus, since the beauty spectrum places light skin tone on its positive side, women are motivated to go in this direction, even when it is not in their own interest. Later in this book, we will see how strategies of adornment contribute to revealing femininity as a fragility, and content men in their phallic status.

When Belliard addresses the concept of skin color as a breach of one's sensitivity, this refers to the psychic envelope, developed in the beginning of life, with the first Ego, originated from the primary physical experience. This Ego was born through the first encounter (the mother), and the mother gave it its value as a limit. This means that this breach is connected to the intimacy of one's mind, and one's deepest conception of oneself as an individual. When one is attacked on this level, one is challenged based on one's self-representation, which emerged from the primary object relationship.

Jean Muteba Rahier (2011) conducted brilliant research in Ecuador on the topic of the hypersexualization of black women in what he calls the Ecuadorian "common sense." He confirms this idea of objectification of black women's bodies being linked to colonization and slavery. The construction of this depreciative representation of black women was always connected to their sexualization and demonization. Rahier reports the dissociation of the terms *mujer* or "woman" and *senora* or "lady," in the ordinary vocabulary. The first refers to a black woman and is often connected to a representation "thought of as being of easy sexual access to men; uncovering her body in public spaces in 'indecent ways;' eventually have sets of children from different men; uneducated and employed as a maid or a cook; her mannerism will be said to be 'un-reined;' her body shape will be voluptuous, almost conceived as being naturally obscene or vulgar" (p. 63). The author adds that the black woman's body is often associated with the representation of the Devil, because of its connection with lust and pleasure, in white men's unconscious.

By contrast, the term "lady" will refer to a white or mixed-race (indigenous and white) woman, and is often connected to a representation as "educated and espouse all the signs of 'social respectability;' viewed as being dedicated to having children and will not be associated—in male conversations—with sexual pleasure; her body will be well covered and never exposed in the public space; (…) Her sexuality is not exposed on the public space. She is 'pure' maternity. She almost seems to have children without engaging in sexual intercourse. Her icon is the Virgin Mary, the Mother of Christ" (p. 63).

Thus, as Rahier notes, the depreciation of black women's bodies not only touches her skin color but also her body parts, especially her buttocks. This representation generates the idea of them as sexually available and allows disrespect. Indeed, the recent development of justice procedure in the United States (Cineas, 2021) has shown how little effort was made to protect young black women from sexual aggression. Because they are hypersexualized, they are less likely to be considered as victims of sexual assault.

In this perspective, it is no wonder that lighter skin could be seen as a strategy to have better opportunities, especially if it continues to be promoted. In Senegal, several campaigns have been launched to valorize natural black skin as the model of beauty, and dermatologists have spoken out to warn people against the damages of skin bleaching products ("Nu Wax Ci with Dr. Hadi Hakim," 2019).[4] Nevertheless, the industry continues to develop and advertise newer types of ingredients, or newer names for them, as soon as the previous one starts to be known as unsafe.

Another aspect that we will discuss in this section is the topic of hairstyle. African traditional braids are still popular, but the trend of wigs and hair extensions has inundated the market, making them a regular hairstyle.

In sub-Saharan Africa, we can imagine that because black people are the most numerous in the population, they are less likely to suffer racial discrimination of any kind. However, beauty criteria set during colonization and supported by the media are still in place. The stigmatization of kinky hair has not been as strong as in Western countries, but, nonetheless, hair straightening has been seen as fashionable and elegant. Recently, however, people had developed an interest in natural African hairstyles and the economic world has followed up with hair salons and equipment, adapted to this lifestyle. The concept of natural black hair being unprofessional is fading, and the Afro haircut inspired by the American icon Angela Davis and the Black Power movement appears to be more and more casual in the public place. New generations and the development of cancer and other diseases have had the reactional effect of promoting natural ways of life, and the use of local products, thus evolving toward a chemical-free lifestyle and therefore putting aside chemical hair relaxers. The trend of dreadlocks has also spread and is no longer connected to the Rastafari lifestyle.

Nevertheless, hairstyle retains a political meaning that not everyone is willing to engage. Indeed, women's clothing and hairstyles have been at the center of social attention for so long that a differentiation from classic models can be seen as reactional, controversial, and political. Society expects justification for women's choices, as if it could never be a preference but automatically the declaration of an opposition.

[4] "Nu Wax Ci avec Dr. Hadi Hakim," published on YouTube on December 28, 2009, retrieved on August 1, 2022 https://www.youtube.com/watch?v=dSvF%2D%2DA0LRY

We must note that, in our study of African tales, we have found that Mami Wata's image is supposed to correspond to this representation of the sexually attractive woman, with light skin tone and long hair. This representation and her association with sex workers confirm this idea of hypersexualization, and personification of men's desire. We have seen earlier that lighter-skinned women are seen as closer to models of beauty and that they are considered more attractive, but also more seductive. The whole industry of skin lightening is based on this hypothesis. Thus, we can imagine that in West Africa, dark skin is closer to the representation of purity and nature. The opposition between the seductive woman and the benevolent mother is visible again in this context. In both cases, men's opinion and tastes are supposedly central and decisive in women's decisions, because their definition evolves in accordance with men's desires. This demonization of black women in the Western context is opposed to a demonization of light-skinned emancipated women, looking more like European women, in African countries. Indeed, it seems that from one side or the other, the representation of the sexual woman is in question, and blamed, but always representing the other extreme, at the center of men's desires. What seems to be less seductive is the idea of emancipation, as it cancels men's exclusive ability to provide for women. Therefore, we can see here that what is at stake is not only the representation of men and women as sexual beings attracted to one another, but more likely the relationship of power, placing one of them above the other. As Foucault wrote, "discourses on sex did not multiply apart from or against power, but in the very space and as the means of its exercise" (1978: 32).

In the next section, we will see how the concept of alterity has evolved and was developed. Then we will try to point out how this dissociation appearing in every dimension of women's representation is connected to alterity, narcissism, and primary object relationship.

5.1.3 Alterity in Psychoanalysis

To understand and describe the concept of alterity, we will start by defining narcissism. The psychoanalytic theory is largely built around this concept, as it is a central aspect in the construction of psychism. Narcissism plays an important role in the Lacanian mirror stage, which is a major phase of early development, determining the relation of the subject with their own image and relationship with others. Gorog (2018) summarizes Lacan's theory: the subject's Ego is secondary to what they perceive in the Other, to the libidinal investment and to the signifiers that come to him from the Other; the Ego is the submission to our own image we find in the Other. This perspective already constitutes a difference from Freudian's theory. The idea of a submission to the image indicates that the base, the matrix of the armature, is relative to a point of support in the Other. Thus, our own construction, and the base of our personality, comes from the Other. Indeed, our mere construction of self is built through the representation we grasp from the primary interaction.

The concept of primary narcissism refers to archaic encounter with the first object, introjected as self, through a narcissistic primary illusion, making it possible for the subject to invest the object as his own self. This appears in the early phases of development, when the mother instantly provides for the newborn, confirming this illusion of infinity and omnipotence. Winnicott (1956) named this "maternal disposition," the primary maternal preoccupation. This context allows the baby to start creating his own Self through the reflection of the Other, reassembling himself around a first feeling of identity.

According to Jung (2015):

> In other words, and paradoxically, the subject finds/creates themself where they are reflected by the object, the identity is found/created from the reciprocity of the duplicate investments that circulate within the primitive dyad. The object investment coincides here with the self investment.
>
> The object investment in the mode of found/created supports in this sense, a first harmonization of the registers of the same and the other, it transitionalizes the two currents of primary narcissism by allowing a work of assimilation of otherness and responses of the object to the self. These answers will have to be in conformity with the logics of the primary narcissism, which they contribute at the same time to set up: ignorance of the

object's otherness, illusion to be at the origin of their own satisfaction, experience of continuity within the environment, etc.[5] (p. 82).

Hence, narcissism allows the baby to find themselves in the mother and illusionarily monopolize parts of her, and thus our personality is intrinsically constructed from the interaction with the first other, in other words, the Maternal Other. Our self-representation takes shape in that encounter, and we can imagine that every future relationship is influenced by our self-representation, and then by this primary encounter.

Then in a second phase, when the baby can understand their wholeness, and build a complete representation of itself, the representation of an object duality naturally emerges, as both internal and external. The baby evolves toward the mirror stage, where they become able to dissociate from the mother, and create objectal relationships. In that last phase, another level of alterity appears, as symbolic. Jung defines this as "produced by the activity of symbolization, closely linked to the process of introjection. We can say that symbolic alterity supposes, unlike imaginary alterity, the recognition by the subject of an independent alterity foreign to himself as well as the access to the representation of absence, in other words to the renunciation to 'representing everything'. It is this limit that allows the subject to represent himself that he does not represent all of himself, to imagine that a part of the object and/or of himself is inaccessible to him."[6]

---

[5]Translated from original quote in French: "Autrement dit, et paradoxalement, le sujet se trouve / crée lui-même là où il est reflété par l'objet, l'identité est trouvée / créée à partir de la réciprocité des investissements en double qui circulent au sein de la dyade primitive. L'investissement de l'objet coïncide ici avec l'investissement de soi.

L'investissement de l'objet sur le mode du trouvé / créé soutient en ce sens une première harmonisation des registres du même et de l'autre, il transitionnalise les deux courants du narcissisme primaire en permettant un travail d'assimilation de l'altérité et des réponses de l'objet au moi. Ces réponses devront être conformes aux logiques du narcissisme primaire, qu'elles contribuent dans le même temps à mettre en place: méconnaissance de l'altérité de l'objet, illusion d'être à l'origine de sa propre satisfaction, éprouvé de continuité avec le monde environnant, etc."

[6]Translated from original quote in French: "une altérité produite par l'activité de symbolisation, étroitement liée au processus d'introjection. On peut dire que l'altérité symbolique suppose, à la différence de l'altérité imaginaire, la reconnaissance par le sujet d'une altérité indépendante et étrangère à soi ainsi que l'accès à la représentation de l'absence, autrement dit au renoncement à 'tout représenter'. C'est cette limite qui permet au sujet de se représenter qu'il ne se représente pas, de se représenter qu'une part de l'objet et / ou de lui-même lui échappe."

This third phase describes the realization of the symbolic alterity in the subject's representation. This second major encounter will represent the absence and signify the true limit to the subject's image; it appears to the subject as a silent observer that has preceded any kind of exchange. This alterity is exterior to both the subject and the mother, ranking them lower in the hierarchy. It is the Great Other. It determines a larger space, where the subject can design a symbolic relationship to themselves uniting and separating them from the object, and in that context, the object is finally considered and perceived as its own identity, different from the subject, and autonomous. The Great Other is the witness to all interactions.

Assoun (2019), when explaining the concept of the Great Other, underlines its importance in the mirror stage, where its gaze validates the subject's existence (p. 65). The Great Other is the space that constitutes the talking subject with their listener. Assoun discusses the concepts of desire, need, and demand: "The need, the demand and the desire are thus aimed at the Other. The demand shows the subjection of the need to the demand, its fundamental alienation. It is the relation to the demand for love that institutes the Other. It is through the passage from demand to desire that the desire of the Other is constituted. This relation is only possible through the mediation of the phallus, the signifier of desire"[7] (p. 66).

The Great Other is therefore the one that is watching, and in this position, it is the phallus inaccessible to the subject and representing the unattainable satisfaction and explaining the existence of the desire. The desire is born from the representation of absence, as the subjects realize their lack. The Name-of-the-Father is a representative of this Great Other as it symbolizes this authority. The representation seems to echo the Freudian concept of phallus being masculine. However, Lacan introduces a significative nuance when he implies the possibility that the father might be a conception, representing the Maternal Other (Foreword to *L'Éveil du printemps*, 1974, AE, 563). In that case, this would be an interesting explanation of this ambivalence toward the mother and women in general.

[7] "Le besoin, la demande et le désir sont donc visés de l'Autre. La demande montre l'assujettissement du besoin à la demande, son aliénation foncière. C'est le rapport à la demande d'amour qui institue l'Autre. C'est par le passage de la demande au désir que se constitue le désir de l'Autre. Ce rapport n'est possible que par la médiation du phallus, signifiant du désir (supra, P. 41)."

Moreover, the Maternal Other being the seducer, the powerful phallic figure, is represented in Melanie Klein's archaic maternal superego. In this last Lacanian representation, it is not the Other that changes, but the subject in their capacity to represent it. Dissociating these figures might be the way culture has chosen to navigate between them and integrate law.

Thus, returning to women's image, because the gaze of the Other was there from the origin, the primary narcissism, where the Ego was created, this would explain how Ego-Skin contains this bodily component. It echoes this double representation, both internal and external, bringing the subject to project his fears onto the other. The subject's representation is defined by the other's gaze because they came to know their own image through alterity; every other encounter is another mirror recalling primary interactions. Therefore, we can hypothesize that people, in their relationship to the Other, reenact the primary relationship and, through the ambivalent figures of femininity, relive this primary dissociation between the Maternal Other and the Great Other. In a woman's imaginary, the destructive woman is opposed to the benevolent mother in a movement where the woman expresses her desire on one side and submits to the order on the other side. In the next chapter, we will see how the masquerade is a strategy for them to fake submission, while exploiting their seductive assets. For now, in the rest of this chapter, we will focus on social aspects of women's lives, and strategies developed using adornment to appear in the public space.

5.2 Adornment as a Method of Social Recognition

5.2.1 Social Stigma and Women's Aesthetic

Because of their gender, women face multiple stereotypes, and we have seen earlier that black women face additional stereotypes putting them at the intersection of several discriminations. In this section, we will discuss the impact of these stereotypes on women's status.

When Devereux (1973) wrote about young female sexual offenders, he described their clothing as excessive and seductive:

> To conclude, we will observe that, nowadays, the excesses of clothing suggesting a false availability have ceased to be the prerogative of the only delinquent woman. There was a time when one could distinguish at first sight the young woman or respectable girl from the street girl. And fifty years ago, it was even possible to distinguish between two equally 'respectable' young people, the young wife or the (single) girl, because the latter was dressed without any research (in the simplest way), almost always in pastel colors, and wore neither jewelry, nor make-up.
>
> These times are long gone because today, the so-called virtuous women or girls have borrowed from the women of lesser virtue not only their secrets of seduction in clothing but even their recipes for body cleanliness. This process is only one of many aspects of a form of cultural osmosis between distinct classes, characteristic of disintegrating societies where, as Sorokin has shown, the upper classes tend to appropriate certain cultural traits and behavioral patterns of the lower classes.[8] (1973, p. 207)

This passage is representative of stigma that women have been facing in the past and still suffer nowadays. Devereux seems to be associating this process with "disintegrating societies," meaning that women would be guarantors of the world's evolution. So, here again, in this author's conception we can underline this idea of conservative societies relying on women to maintain cultural codes, against the anxiety that their world could collapse. Women's clothing supposedly determined their status and categorized them by level of respectability. However, it seems that this

[8] Translated from original quote in French: "Pour en finir, on observera que, de nos jours, les excès vestimentaires suggérant une fausse disponibilité ont cessé d'être l'apanage de la seule femme délinquante. Il était un temps où l'on pouvait distinguer de prime abord la jeune femme ou fille respectable de la fille des rues. Et il y a cinquante ans, il était même possible de distinguer entre deux jeunes personnes également "respectables", la jeune épouse de la jeune fille, car celle-ci était vêtue sans recherche aucune, presque toujours dans des teintes pastels, et ne portait ni bijoux, ni maquillage.

Ces temps sont bien révolus car, aujourd'hui, les femmes ou filles dites vertueuses ont emprunté aux femmes de petite vertu non seulement leurs secrets de séduction vestimentaire mais jusqu'à leurs recettes de propreté corporelle. Ce processus n'est qu'un parmi nombre d'autres aspects d'une forme d'osmose culturelle entre classes distinctes, caractéristique des sociétés en voie de désintégration où, comme l'a démontré Sorokin, les classes supérieures ont tendance à s'approprier certains traits culturels et certains modèles de comportement des classes inférieures."

scenario has already changed at the time of this statement, and we can imagine that they are different now. Nevertheless, this representation of dissociation between the pure young girl/respectable married woman, and the sexually attractive woman appears along these lines.

In Senegal, Fatou Diop has conducted research on Senegalese people's expenses on and behavior toward clothing and has found that traditional clothing is an expression of cultural identity, and a sign of opposition to the exogenous colonial culture. Clothing is not only an individual choice, but also expresses the collective attitude to promote a political message of cultural valuation.

> In a country where everyone, individually or collectively, is in search of a social "elsewhere", clothing is presented as an imaginary territory (the Senegalese outfit) where an identity, also imaginary (to be a real Senegalese) is composed in an ambiguous way through a reference to an imaginary community (the country, Senegal). (Diop, 2013b, p. 122)

Awa Thiam confirmed this return to the traditional Senegalese outfit (2014, p. 36), and noted a change from the past because older and more conservative women used to be the ones valuing traditional clothing, whereas modern women would embrace European outfits. Nowadays, traditional clothing has evolved in many directions and proposes a diversity of choices for different types of clients.

Diop also noted the mystical properties of traditional clothing. Indeed, in some ethnic settings it is thought to protect from ill fate and the evil eye (2013b, p. 123). During pregnancy, women are advised to wear traditional clothing covering their belly, to hide it from envious eyes. The same rule applies to newlyweds, and young people undergoing initiation rituals.

Hence, clothes are a second layer of protection, and connect people to a cultural group to reaffirm their identity. This reinvestment of cultural identity, which Fatou Diop interprets as a collective opposition to colonialism, has an impact on social representations of beauty. Moreover, this trend and diversification of products in the field of traditional clothing among young people may encourage pride and empowerment. It reveals people's willingness to promote local fabrics and create their own style.

However, some research in Congo (Moulemvo, 2011) and Senegal (Bredeloup, 2016) has noted the effects of massive importation of second-hand clothes on micro-enterprises and local sewers. This business has globalized people into a common international dress code. However, in Senegal, the return to traditional clothing shows a willingness to claim cultural identity and detach from this globalization. In Diop's paper (2013b), interviewees explain their preference for traditional clothing as stemming from their concern for decency and body coverage. Women especially justify this preference by the desire to appear more decent, particularly regarding their religion. European clothing can be associated with acculturation and be less covering and tighter than traditional African clothes. One might think that this last point also explains that women face more judgment when wearing imported clothes because then they suffer the stereotypes addressed to their European counterparts, as being more open to seduction.

Thus, women's appearance is always used against them while society puts pressure on them to comply with specific aesthetic rules. Isabel Boni-Le Goff (2019) has written about women in the corporate world of consultants in France. This article, even though it is not written about our target population, does explain some interesting mechanisms at work in our field. Indeed, Boni-Le Goff reports how women in the corporate world are watched and criticized on their clothing; they face the dilemma of either "being a bimbo or a lesbian." In other words, they cannot dress up using too many feminine accessories, fearing being considered flirtatious, and when they are not feminine enough, they are called "lesbians," as a dismissive comment on their lack of attractiveness. Boni-Le Goff has found that many women in this environment have resolved this dilemma through the construction of their own dress code, and the addition of adornment (earrings, jewels, head scarves, bags, etc.). Through adornment, they have taken control of their image and redesigned their relationship with seduction, pushing away this sexualized representation, while retaining their femininity. As the author says, they have built a "professional mask," a "masquerade femininity," to find their way into this masculine professional environment.

Enlightened by Boni-Le Goff's interpretation, we can imagine that the new generation of African stylists and designers of modern clothes and accessories inspired by original traditional style are also reacting to stigma and creating their own dress code. This would be a response to the two stereotypes they are facing: firstly, to be too far removed from their African heritage and secondly to be insufficiently dressed and show too much of their curves. Indeed, Diop reported several testimonies stating that people who wear traditional clothes are more likely to be respected, and considered decent, than those wearing European clothes.

Another aspect of the development of African designers is their reception in Western countries. Pascale Berloquin-Chassany (2006) has investigated the topic of African creators, and the reception of the "ethnic" label in France. According to this author, the process of labeling black designers as "ethnic" is independent of their creations, as they are considered as such and so are their productions, no matter what style they choose. Here is another stereotype that African people will face on their path. They are expected to represent a specific image and are marketed as exotic. The creation and development of new brands demonstrating diversity of lifestyles and accessories can contribute to controlling their image, and show more of their artistic identity, instead of others' expectations.

We have interviewed some young West African women who have created their own clothing, accessory, and jewelry brands.

Fatita (40) and Tabara (39) have created a jewelry brand called Imaara:

> We were inspired by African jewels, we used to see our parents and grandparents wearing some jewels that were not in the current trend. We had some of those that we liked but did not wear ourselves. We were inspired by those creations, we tried to modernize them, to bring our personal touch, to address this new generation of African women who love jewels and want to wear locally made accessories. Our first inspirational jewel was the Baule bead, and we have worked on this piece to offer a variety of colors associating it with pearls. We also have identified other African pieces that we would like to develop in further collections. What matters is the possibility to wear those African pieces casually to go to work for example, so new generations can take the most of that heritage.
>
> There has been a boom in the field of fashion in Africa, and more and more African women, want to buy locally made fashion products. With our brand, and the other designers displaying their products in our shop, we are proud to be able to deliver that, in Africa and abroad.

In this testimony, we can notice that the concepts of transmission and modernity are central. The designers are committed to promote locally made products that convey original pieces of heritage, with their personal touch, to address the taste of the new generation.

Rabiaa (39) has created a brand of clothes and leather goods called Kundi:

> I wanted to produce goods of high quality, to show that it is possible to have that in Africa and locally made. As a woman I believe that we have the power to fight injustices, and we must fight them. We should all be aware that we are able to do the same as men, even more. In the community women should support one another, not all of us are aware of their potential. Until we all do, we will not be able to evolve.
>
> About the stigma on women, I believe we as women always want to be attractive, and to love ourselves the way we are, it takes a lot of self-consciousness and personal strength. Beauty standards of light skin women with European hair, have existed for too long, and people have gotten used to believe that they are all there is, it is very difficult to get rid of them. Everyone can contribute to fight those stereotypes, starting in their own house with their daughters, teaching them to love themselves as they are.

This second testimony emphasizes cultural pride and identity. Rabiaa in her project as a designer is an ambassador of women's development. She promotes an ideal of professionalism to fight stereotypes of African products lacking quality. Additionally, she promotes a better representation of black women in our speech and education, for the next generation to not convey these beauty standards.

In the next section, we will explore in detail how religion is also influencing their clothing and then we will observe how this department can also be a coping strategy to manage their appearance and introduce a nuance to how people look at them.

5.2.2 Religious Aestheticism and Identity

Senegalese authors have noted Senegalese women's growing tendency to adopt the Muslim veil (Mbow (2001), Thiam (2014)). In Western countries, the Muslim veil is a question of gender, politics, and community. In this section, we will discuss its representation for African women and examine its symbolism.

As Penda Mbow notes, there has been a growing number of Senegalese women who have started to wear the Muslim veil in public. The author raises this point to note how it is not culturally a part of Senegalese heritage, but rather an importation from Arabic countries. Moreover, we discussed in the previous section this distancing from Westernization, and this movement can be seen as a result.

The Muslim veil is a controversial topic, because on the one hand, it may show how women choose to subtract themselves from the diktat of beauty making their body available to the gaze of society, without their consent; on the other hand, it may be interpreted as the domination of the feminine gender by the patriarchy. This problematic is located at a delicate intersection that gives it a political and social dimension, even though it could have remained a personal individual question.

The veil raises important questions in psychoanalysis about women's bodies and adornment. Before discussing its religious value, we will analyze its symbolism. According to Anne Juranville (2004), the veil does not hide or protect, but designates an impossible place, one that halts the representation, which there finds its origin. She draws on the concept of castration to describe its symbolism. We will come back to her explanation in the next chapter. For now, we will focus on the dimensions of hiding and masking that the veil can convey, and its capacity to represent maturity, wisdom, and belonging.

In our previous research (Diop, 2012), while working with women after hysterectomy and breast mastectomy, we gathered testimonies of several Senegalese women, declaring how often they wore the veil after their operation. In Chap. 7, we will analyze their testimonies in detail, but in this section we will try to grasp the symbolism of the veil in their remarks. Patients mentioned two reasons:

- Some said that they felt like it was easier to cover their synthetic prothesis under their clothes, with the veil, because it had the effect of a blurred layer. Therefore, they bought a collection of fancy veils that they could match with their outfits. Additionally, they felt proud to

adopt the religious veil because they did not have the motivation to do so in the past, and this situation had made it easier.
- Others said that after their operation, they felt like they were more mature and wanted to express this through the addition of the veil to their outfit. They felt motivated to gain more knowledge of their religion, and because of this difficult experience they had been through, they were more spiritual and faithful.

Regarding the first reason, we may think of the veil as a feminine accessory, connected to spirituality, and renewing the outfit. This change will capture the gaze of others, while masking the operation. Women wearing the veil for this reason choose what they offer to the other's gaze. They do not want to be associated with pain and illness due to their mastectomy, so they create another style and image. In short, if people are going to look at them, they want to know how and why, using the veil as an accessory. Enveloping their image is narcissizing and helps them get through the postoperative stage, to accept their new body. Because the veil is connected to Islam, wearing it makes them pure and provides a positive image, reinforcing this narcissization. We should add that this process of narcissization is not to be interpreted as pathological, but rather a coping strategy to regain balance after a traumatic incident.

Women wearing the veil for the second reason put more emphasis on its symbolic value as a mark of religious maturity. Indeed, they were invested in religion as a postoperation project, to grow out of this phase with more knowledge, and rebuilt themselves in a more powerful position. Being wiser and more mature was a smart way to contrast with the impression that others would look at them with pity and consider them inferior. In this situation, they were also in a process of renarcissization, using the veil and their religious practice to turn their life around and become powerful in the face of the illness that made them feel out of control and powerless.

Thus, in these situations, we have seen how the veil as an accessory of adornment allows women to gain narcissism in the fact that it summons the Great Other as the supreme witness to women's fitness. This accessory of adornment gives them power and creates a potential space of becoming. When worn as a cover, the veil masks the lack and hides the weaknesses, but when it is worn as an accessory, it enhances seduction, entertains the gaze and underlines the powerful status. In both cases, the lack is actualized in the reality of the operation, as a real castration. When women wearing the veiled take a position of seduction or power, they impersonate the masquerade femininity, making the veil as an accessory, the symbol of their disguise.

One of the designers we interviewed for the previous section wears the Muslim veil, and we asked her about her interpretation of it. According to Rabiaa (39 years old):

> For me the veil is a symbol of protection, to me wearing it today has a very spiritual connection; along with clothes that cover my chest and body, it protects me from other's malevolent intentions.

This testimony is confirmed in Fatou Diop's study, where she collected testimonies evoking the protection of the veil used to cover one's hair. Her participants reported that it could protect from malevolent eyes, and jealousy. We can imagine that women in our study have chosen to wear the veil for similar reasons, to protect themselves from further attacks. Indeed, they may have perceived the illness as somehow an attack representing their vulnerability to others. Here, the veil is a protection used to cover and shield.

Another aspect of this question of the Muslim veil resides in its representation as opposed to women's emancipation. Indeed, the political conflict is circumscribed in this topic. Wallon and Derghal-Hammoudi (2009) interviewed Iranian women and reported their opinions on the obligation for the veil in their country. They found that the new generation no longer sees it as a religious accessory, but more like an instrument of oppression with no connection to religion as they see it. The authors observe how the veil in this case underlines the object of desire, while paradoxically showing part of the hair in a seductive manner.

Others in the field of gender (Sanna and Varikas 2011; Sanna 2011) seek to dissociate the question of feminism from the topic of the Muslim veil, because they consider it to be an extrapolation of colonialism, representing veiled women as opposed to emancipation and pathologizing them. In the next section, we will see how this question can be approached through a decolonized lens.

5.2.3 Decolonizing Women's Body

Shose Kessi and Floretta Boonzaier (2018) have developed Lugones's (2011) theory about decolonial feminist psychology and applied it to research in psychology. They "propose that a decolonial feminist project for psychology centers questions of institutional racism, embodiment and space, identity-related impact of segregation and exclusion from access to resources and centers of power" (2018, p. 75).

Their intent is to "focus on the subjective-intersubjective to reveal that disaggregating oppression disaggregates the subjective-intersubjective springs of colonized women's agency" (2018, pp. 76–77).

They present the concept of "decolonial feminism" as the possibility to overcome the coloniality of gender. Therefore, analyzing colonized women and deploying useful research strategies about them is a development of decolonial feminism. Indeed, our positioning to understand women and determine the symbolic and subjective representation of adornment is one of those developments.

In the previous sections, we have discussed social codes on women's appearance, whether this is classic dress code or religious prescriptions. Both reflect social expectations of women, aiming to validate social authority. Devereux's previously cited paragraph indicated how adornment gathers specific information about marital status. In other words, it shows if a woman is under a man's guard. Thus, women's bodies are the place of men's exchange, representing their assets and values.

Several research studies have been conducted in medicine, objectifying and dehumanizing black women's bodies (Peirreti-Courtis, 2018). Social sciences also has its share of pathologizing colonized women in research. Researchers in decolonial feminist theory invoke a "decolonial intersectional feminist narrative perspective to think carefully about how the narrative we produce as researchers may be taken up to advance particular antitransformative agendas that may further marginalize and disadvantage oppressed groups" (Boonzaier et al., 2019, p. 471). Indeed, researchers willing to question women's problematics may pathologize them when comparing their lifestyles to European ways of life. Using the example of the veil is demonstrative of how a political conflict can be extended and misplaced on women's bodies and represent the opposition of two visions. This political opposition places women's bodies on the war field without questioning their ability to make their own judgments, independent of their personal positioning in the conflict.

When discussing emancipation, some people have the social representation of sexual emancipation, and European dress code, whereas others will refer to economic emancipation, unlinked to sexuality. These representations transpire in research, because as Mary Putman Jacobi wrote:

> Psychological knowledge is socially situated, that is, that interpretations of data reflect the perspectives and intentions of the researcher.

Thus, even in research, the evolution of perspectives follows that of society. Researchers themselves are contextually situated and aim to confirm their own biases. Examining research through a decolonial feminist intersectional lens necessitates the exercise of rethinking biases, and deconstructing our own stereotypes on women, gender, power, dress code, and lifestyle. Devereux in his time could not detach from his own stereotypes on women to analyze the cases of what he called "young female sexual delinquents."

A real difference can appear in the goals of research, being not to describe an issue, but to observe adaptation strategies and offer new perspectives to participants themselves. Boonzaier (in Ugelvik et al. (2019)) has developed practical exhaustive guidelines for research to be useful and culturally relevant to participants.

In the field of medicine, Delphine Peirreti-Courtis (2018) has studied how French doctors in colonial times used to refer to black male and female bodies. According to this author, women were animalized and inferiorized in their descriptions. Those colonizers felt like it was their duty to teach their ways of life and educate colonized populations into their "civilization" and religion. Because of this dehumanization, women's bodies were given taxonomic attention, and medically brutalized, as the story of the Hottentot Venus[9] demonstrates. Recently, Chidiebere Ibe, a medical school student (Bouanchaud, 2022), published a drawing of a pregnant black woman and the fetus inside of her. This representation was highly acclaimed, since it made the viewer realize that all medical images are shown using white bodies. In medicine, black bodies are analyzed as specimens of their difference, and not as regular male or female schemas. As researchers, our duty is to work toward more honesty and democracy in research.

In the field of marketing, and aesthetics, we have seen how colonization has played a large role in shaping the beauty spectrum. Here, when we talk about colonization, we may also refer to domination at large, including how men have ways to put pressure on women. In this context, moving toward decolonization means underlining women's coping strategies, and promoting their ways of reinventing themselves. Hanétha Véthé-Congolo's "femmism" is one of these other ways, because it takes the past into consideration, and points out what women did with what they had, and how they built their own status through lived experiences.

The world is now globalized, and no one can claim to build a new concept with absolutely no influences from preexisting others. However, designers have shown that even though fashion and style are in constant evolution, they can convey cultural traditions while designing original models. Using a decolonized lens allows consideration without comparing, and discovering instead of critiquing. In this movement, the Other is always recalling our own little stranger (this part of strangeness inside us), and our fear of facing it echoes in our reaction to newness. To approach

[9] Sarah Baartman (1789–1815) was an African woman known as the Hottentot Venus. She was taken from South Africa to Europe, and was exploited as an attraction, in mundane and circus spectacles. Her body was retained for racist scientific purposes in France and was only returned to be buried in her homeland in 2002, upon Nelson Mandela's request.

the world through a decolonial perspective, we must start to ask ourselves what we seek in our own studies as researchers, and what purpose we have.

In the next chapter, we will finally introduce, analyze, and discuss the concepts of adornment and masquerade in psychoanalysis. This will allow us to put in perspective everything we have discussed about the Ego-Skin and alterity, with the construction of femininity and beauty.

References

Assoun, P. (2019). Chapitre V. Figures de l'autre. Dans : *Paul-Laurent Assoun éd., Lacan* (pp. 63–69). Paris cedex 14 : Presses Universitaires de France.

Beneduce, R. (2006). *L'apport de Franz Fanon à l'ethnopsychiatrie critique, 1*(89), 85–100.

Berloquin-Chassany, P. (2006). Créateurs africains de mode vestimentaire et labellisation "ethnique" (France, Antilles, Afrique de l'Ouest francophone). *Autrepart, 38*, 173–190. https://doi.org/10.3917/autr.038.0173

Biko, S. (1978). I write what I like. London, England: Bowerdean.

Boni-Le Goff, I. (2019). Des expert·e·s respectables ? Esthétique vestimentaire et production de la confiance. *Travail, genre et sociétés, 41*, 67–86. https://doi.org/10.3917/tgs.041.0067

Boonzaier, F., Fleetwood, J., Presser, L., Sandberg, S. & Ugelvik, T. (Eds.) (2019). *Researching sex work: Doing Decolonial, intersectional narrative analysis* (pp. 467–491). The Emerald Handbook of Narrative Criminology, Emerald Publishing Limited, Bingley. https://doi.org/10.1108/978-1-78769-005-920191037.

Bouanchaud, C. (2022, January, 17). *En représentant un fœtus noir, un étudiant révèle l'invisibilisation de la diversité en médecine.* Le Monde. https://www.lemonde.fr/societe/article/2022/01/14/en-representant-un-f-tus-noir-un-etudiant-revele-l-invisibilisation-de-la-diversite-en-medecine_6109538_3224.html

Bredeloup, S. (2016). Fëgg jaay : fripe business ou fripe éthique au Sénégal? *Mouvements, 87*, 142–154. https://doi.org/10.3917/mouv.087.0142

Carberry, C., & Brooks-Gordon, B. (2020). Black therapist-white families, therapists' perceptions of cultural competence in clinical practice. As cited in Majors R., Carberry K., & Ransaw T.S., *The international handbook of black community mental health*. Emerald Publishing Limited.

Cineas, F. (2021, September 29). *R. Kelly was convicted. Are we finally listening to Black women?* Vox. https://www.vox.com/22698489/r-kelly-conviction-black-women-survivors

Devereux, G. (1973). *Essai d'ethnopsychiatrie générale.* Gallimard.

Diop, C. (2013a, February). *L'épistémologie du point de vue situé à l'épreuve du terrain et de l'académie en France. Restitution d'un parcours de recherche.* Paper presented at the transdisciplinary day of LARHA, Grenoble. Retrieved from https://www.academia.edu/3880184/_Lépistémologie_du_point_de_vue_situé_à_lépreuve_du_terrain_et_de_lacadémie_en_France._Restitution_d_un_parcours_de_recherche_

Diop, F. (2013b). Tradition et comportement de consommation au Sénégal : une étude exploratoire sur la tenue vestimentaire. *La Revue des Sciences de Gestion, 261-262,* 121–130. https://doi.org/10.3917/rsg.261.0121

Diop, I. (2012). *Hystérectomy, mastectomie et statut de la femme au Sénégal* (Doctoral thesis). Université de Rouen.

Dogra, N. (2012). Representations of global poverty: Aid, development and international NGOs. New York, NY: I. B. Taurus.

El Saadawi, N. (1997). The Nawal El Saadawi reader. New York, NY: Zed Books.

Fanon, F. (1986). Black skin, white masks. London, England: Pluto Press (1952-French).

Foucault, M. (1978). *The history of sexuality.* Pantheon Books.

Gordon, L. R. (2015). *What fanon said: A philosophical introduction to his life and thought.* Fordham University Press.

Gorog, J. (2018). Du narcissisme au stade du miroir et retour. La position centrale de la jalousie et l'envie dans la psychanalyse. *Revue des Collèges de Clinique psychanalytique du Champ Lacanien, 17,* 74–88. https://doi.org/10.3917/rccpcl.017.0074

Juranville, A. (2004). Voile, féminin et inconscient. *Adolescence, 223,* 523–532. https://doi.org/10.3917/ado.049.0523

Kanazawa, S. (2006). Mind the gap . . . in intelligence: Reexamining the relationship between inequality and health. British Journal of Health Psychology, 11, 623–642.

Kessi, S., & Boonzaier, F. (2018). Centre/ing decolonial feminist psychology in Africa. *South African Journal of Psychology, 48*(3), 299–309. https://doi.org/10.1177/0081246318784507

Lee A. (2005). *Unconscious bias theory in employment discrimination litigations.*

Lugones, M., (2011). Methodological notes toward a Decolonial feminism. In *Decolonizing epistemologies* (pp. 68–86). Isasi-Diàz, Ada Maria, Published by Fordham University Press.
Mama, A. (1995). Beyond the masks: Race, gender, and subjectivity. New York, NY: Routledge.
Mbow, P. (2001). L'Islam et la femme sénégalaise, Revue négro-africaine de littérature et de philosophie, *Ethiopiques* numéros 66–67, 1er et 2ème semestre, 2001, 7 pages. Publié sur http://ethiopiques.refer.sn
Moulemvo, A. (2011). Importation de vêtements de seconde main et compétitivité des micro-entreprises de couture au Congo-Brazzaville. *Revue Congolaise de Gestion, 14*, 9–33. https://doi.org/10.3917/rcg.014.0009
Nicholas, L. J., & Cooper, S. (1990). Psychology & apartheid. Johannesburg, South Africa: Vision Publications.
Sanna, M. (2011). Ces corps qui ne comptent pas : les musulmanes voilées en France et au Royaume-Uni. *Cahiers du Genre, 50*, 111–132. https://doi.org/10.3917/cdge.050.0111
Sanna, M., & Varikas, E. (2011). Genre, modernité et 'colonialité' du pouvoir : penser ensemble des subalternités dissonantes : Introduction. *Cahiers du Genre, 50*, 515. https://doi.org/10.3917/cdge.050.0005
Shervington, D. (1994). Reflections on African-American resistance to population policies and birth control. In L. A. Mazur (Ed.), Beyond the numbers (pp.281–284). Washington, DC: Island Press.
Spivak, G. C. (1988). Can the subaltern speak. In N. Cary & L. Grossbierg (Eds.), Marxism and the interpretation of culture (pp. 271–313). Urbana, IL: University of Illinois Press.
Thiam, A. (2014). La sexualité féminine africaine en mutation, L'exemple du Sénégal, L'Harmattan.
Véthé-Congolo, H. (2020). Nous sommes martiniquaises, Pawol en bouches de femmes chataîgnes. *Une pensée existentialiste noire sur la question des femmes*, L'Harmattan.
Wallon, E., & Derghal-Hammoudi, N. (2009). Le voile en Iran : la construction d'une nouvelle identité féminine. *L'Autre, 10*, 305–317. https://doi.org/10.3917/lautr.030.0305
Winnicott, D. W. (1956). Primary maternal preoccupation. In L. Caldwell & H. T. Robinson (Eds.), *The Collected Works of D. W. Winnicott: Volume 5, 1955–1959* (New York, 2016; online edn, Oxford Academic, 1 Dec. 2016). https://doi.org/10.1093/med:psych/9780190271374.003.0039

6

Masquerade and Femininity

The concept of womanliness as a masquerade was first brought forward by Joan Riviere in 1929. She used it to describe the attitudesss of a woman she was seeing as a patient. This person was highly educated and was evolving in a professional position where her work consisted in speaking and writing, often giving her the opportunity to make presentations in front of an audience. Her professional ability was confirmed by the quality of her work, and she was accomplished as a woman in her private life. However, at every presentation, she was suffering anxiety and needed reassurance from men in the audience.

To analyze this behavior, Riviere revisited her patient's past and personal relationship with her parents. She found that this woman's father was also in an important position of creating and publishing research, and her relationship with her mother was conflictual. Riviere explains this conflict as related to an unsolved Oedipus complex. The analysis revealed that the woman did not feel secure in her position of knowledge, as if it represented a phallic position she had stolen from her father. The need for reassurance from other men, putting her in a position of weakness, aimed at hiding that she had taken possession of the phallus, thus resulting in this appearance of womanliness.

I. S. Diop, *Adornment, Masquerade and African Femininity*, Pan-African Psychologies,
https://doi.org/10.1007/978-3-031-28748-0_6

Thus, Joan Riviere, when referring to masquerade, asserts that women use this apparent weakness, under the traits of ogling and coquetting, to drive away men's suspicion and fear. This could be a way to avoid their reaction of punishment or rejection. Later, Jacques Lacan took this concept and described it more thoroughly, opposing it to the parade, describing men's' attitude to women. Indeed, Lacan defines the parade as a sort of exaggeration of assurance, displaying an illusory power. Their accomplishment in seduction would be the only way to finally actualize this power.

In this chapter, we will present the concept of masquerade and associate it with that of adornment. First, we will present the concept of female superego, to understand where this fear of the Other comes from. Then in a second development, we will examine the mother–daughter relationship to grasp its uniqueness as the first confrontation with the Maternal Other. Later, we will address multiple developments of the concept of masquerade, as an adaptation strategy for women to navigate into society without raising fear and aggressiveness from men eager to maintain their social privilege. And finally, we will link this concept to the whole scope of this study, as a symbolic representation: the coexistence of the two primary Others, combined figures of Omnipotence in women. We will see how, because women are the conjunction of the two Others, relationships with them are eternal reproductions of primary interactions, actualizing intense archaic content and triggering primary anxieties. This can explain the energy society puts into codifying relationships with women and between them. Therefore, adornment would be a masquerade, to hide that symbolic representation and its implicit ramifications.

6.1 Masquerade and the Game of Power

6.1.1 Perspectives of the Feminine Oedipus and Superego

According to Freud, girls' and boys' Oedipus complexes are played in a mirror (1917, p. 12). This means that the girl wants to have the boy's penis, and the desire to have children is a sublimation of this desire and is represented as a destiny, an ambition of achievement. In short, this desire for a child exists to compensate for the lack of penis which the girl child is supposedly suffering from. This representation seems to be simply deducted from the masculine Oedipus and is based upon the reasoning that girls have the same representation of phallus as boys, and that phallus actually refers to what Freud calls it. These two assumptions are not verified, and the family constellation where this configuration takes place is the nuclear family. This narrows down even more the applicability of this theory, excluding most African and Afro descendant women, coming from extended families, raised with other parental figures than their parents (aunts and uncles, siblings, grandparents). Melanie Klein's representation of the Oedipus complex seems more realistic to us, since it considers the mother–baby interaction as central and addresses triangulation as the determining phase of the Oedipus complex. We have seen in Jacqueline Rabain's work in Senegal, previously mentioned in this book, how this triangulation introduces the father, and the role of the family as horizontal buffers for the actors (mother, father, baby). What this configuration has also taught us is how society gives meaning and substance to the child's reaction, paving the way for the acquisition of language. Jacques Lacan has indeed given great importance to language as fundamental to the structuration of psychism, through which the child is invited to escape the risk of a destructive fusional primary relationship. Thus, as evoked earlier, the child considers the Maternal Other as omnipotent and the sole owner of everything they want, but the confrontation with the social order puts them in a position of witness to the mother's castration, and erection of a greater figure: the Great Other, represented by the real father.

According to Lacan, the child's desire is for the phallus and not the penis itself (1958). He situates the origin of this desire in the primary object relation, as a projection of the desire originally aiming at the Other. Through nursing and care, the mother integrates and gives meaning to her child's sensations; in this way she assumes the existence of a desire in projection of her own and seeks to respond to it. The child enjoys this response and the maternal love offered to them, and the mother sees it as a testimony of recognition. From then on, the child is put in the position of being able to desire, through the mediation of a demand directed to the Other.

This demand is never really fulfilled and leaves a circumscribed void that eternally seeks to be satisfied. Lacan describes the object *a* as "an object that produces lack and is at the origin of desire." It is the "lack to be" that is situated beyond the demand and signifies an inscription of the subject, in an endless relation to the Other's desire (Dor, 1985, p. 189), and thus it is identified with the phallic object. During the Oedipal phase, the child abandons this position, to place himself as a desiring subject, and in this way, "they find substitutive objects of desire coming metonymically in place of the lost object" (Dor, 1985, p. 189). The subject acquiring the status of desiring subject is a positive resolution of the Oedipus complex; it is made possible on condition that both real and imaginary mothers (maternal imago that the girl has internalized) agree to let go. Thus, they let the child be connected to the Great Other and accept Reality and Law.

Numerous authors have taken an interest in the concept of female superego, but here we will concentrate only on the works of Catherine Millot (1984) and Hanns Sachs (1984). Later in this work, we will discuss their relevance in our cultural context. For Millot, the girl retains the castration complex, only to overcome it late and incompletely. This impacts the construction of the female superego, which is compromised, because of its opposition to the girl's Oedipal desire toward her father. Sachs insists on the concept of girls' renunciation of the Oedipal relation. Indeed, according to him, the frustration generated by this renunciation of the oral desire directed toward the father is the origin of the construction of the female superego.

Thus, the superego will be formed only after renunciation, leaving the girl with a dependence on a real Other, which can be the father, or most often a substitute. The anguish of loss settles in this relation to the Other, like an "end of non-receipt of her phallic request" (Millot, 1984, p. 116). To fight this anguish of loss, the girl faces the possibly limitless demands of this Other, positioning herself in place of this superego that she lacks. Thus, according to Millot, the female superego comes from the outside, and a maternal Ego ideal is formed in reaction to maternal castration, maintaining the mother in her omnipotent status (p. 118). Thus, every relationship where the girl formulates a demand would be a new occasion for this Maternal Other to actualize fear and anxiety, and because of this external origin of the superego, the gaze of society remains a determinant for the narcissistic construction, as relays of the Other. For this reason, masquerade could be a response strategy to fill that eternally gaping void.

Nevertheless, Jessica Choukroun (2014, p. 152) asks, "if there is no exit from the Oedipus for the girl, no identity foundation for her to find with the father, how do we let go of this pre-oedipal mother who originated a demand for exclusive love?" Liliane Abensour (2011) finds an answer to this question, when she evokes the existence of a "wild maternal" connected to the violence of motherhood, ranged on the side of pure impulses, freed upon the moment of childbirth. This maternal, wild and cruel, is even difficult to apprehend for analysts because of its horror. What makes this reaction so wild is its archaism, and the opportunity to finally fill in that void at the source of every desire. However, according to Abensour, most of the time, mothers sublimate this excessive impulse movement through counterinvestments found in childcare. This brings us back to the concept of care, and appearance. From the early stages, children are cared for, and their physical appearance is at the center of their caregiver's preoccupation. If that first mirror is the Maternal Other, under the traits of the real caregiver, backed with that representation of an archaic destructive force, we can imagine how our image and narcissism is impacted by Other. Additionally, coming back to adornment, we can imagine how our appearance reflects fragments of our self-representation. Therefore, we can assume that women's adornment reflects more than just their tastes. Indeed, it could be some kind of transitional space, where they can express anxieties of this primary relationship, and solve specific psychological conflicts.

I believe that this horrific avatar, overlapping the loving and caring representation of the mother, is what remains of the archaic maternal superego, in the collective unconscious. It transcribes into the figure of the devouring mother. This female figure is well described by Amadou Hampathé Bâ (2004) in the tale of Njeddo Dewal, a witch sent by God to punish humans for their perversion. She has seven beautiful daughters, serving as bait to attract suitors, whose blood she feeds on. Her daughters are devoted to her, and their hymens are constantly regenerated after each union, so that they can never become wives, women, or mothers. The witch refuses to give up her youth, her sexuality, and to give way to her daughters by opposing the order of generations. Bâgoumawel, the precocious child, born from a lonely marginalized mother, will defeat the witch to save his people. In this tale, the hero's mother embodies the figure of the benevolent mother and has a predominant place, because by her love and her abnegation, she reinforces her son's personality and encourages his singularity, conducting him to fulfil his destiny (self-provoked birth, early acquisition of language, self-naming, self-feeding, and early walking), in order to restore the Law of men by condemning the devouring mother at the origin of symbolic castration. If Bâgoumawel is the only one able to defeat the witch, it is because he is excluded from the circuit of exchanges, and escapes the symbolic law, like other heroes of mythology. Because he was never in a position of desire, he is out of the Maternal Other's reach, and stays out of the Other's gaze. This tale shows how the two Others are in question here and their dysregulation causes chaos. The precocious child is needed to reset the world and build a new order.

According to Jacqueline Schaeffer (2015), one of the premises for the object relation is the mother's action of keeping her daughter, not from the father's desire, but her own jouissance, and the primary scene, thus preparing her for her encounter with a lover in the future. The erection of the penis as a symbol of phallus allows a distancing from the pregenital omnipotent maternal imago and maternal hold.

Schaeffer comments on Abensour's concept of "wild maternal" cited previously. It must be disguised by myths, phantasies, and symbols to be approached, but also kept at a secure distance.

6.1.2 Mother–Daughter Relationship, the Experience of *Ravage*

The relationship between mother and daughter has been the subject of several explorations in psychoanalysis. Yolande Govindama sees an ambivalence in this relationship, linking it to the notion of symbolic permutation (2011, p. 124). Indeed, the girl's entry into puberty activates a mirror game that sends the mother back to her place as a daughter and to the experience of primary jouissance in front of the Maternal Other. Lacan (1974) qualifies this experience of *ravage* and Marie-Magdeleine Lessana defines it as follows (2000, p. 12): "the *ravage* between daughter and mother is not a duel, nor the sharing of a good, it is the experience which consists in giving body to the torturing, deaf hatred, present in the exclusive love between them, by the expression of direct aggressiveness. The '*ravage*' is played between the two women touched with the image of splendor of a woman's body desired by a man. It reveals the impossible harmony of their love clashing with the impossible sexual activity between them."[1]

The father's role in this relation is to occupy his function as third, "to be the port where the young girl would take refuge to protect herself from the swells and swirls of this exclusive ravaging love with her mother"[2] (Lessana, 2000, p. 8). This function as third is supposed to support the girl in the acquisition of her identity and the appropriation of her body. Thanks to him, she can withdraw from her mother's projections and make her body exist through the experience of the Other jouissance. Thus, the symbolic permutation is operated through this game of projection-subtraction-transmission and weaves itself like the red thread of generations of women. It is in this that Lyasmine Kessaci considers ravaging as a specific mode of mother–daughter transmission (Kessaci, 2015, p. 100).

By observing the models of Wolof society, we can see how the paternal function is not one of care, but rather of authority, so much so that mothers are the guarantors of the affection given to children. The duality of the parental couple added to the mediation of the larger family is expressed through these roles: the father as guarantor of society's prohibitions, the

---

[1] Translated from original quote in French: "le ravage entre fille et mère n'est pas un duel, ni le partage d'un bien, c'est l'expérience qui consiste à donner corps à la haine torturante, sourde, présente dans l'amour exclusif entre elles, par l'expression d'une agressivité directe. Le ravage se joue entre les deux femmes touchées par l'image de splendeur d'un corps de femme désiré par un homme. Il révèle l'impossible harmonie de leur amour qui se heurte à l'impossible activité sexuelle entre elles."

[2] Translated from original quote in French: "d'être le port où la petite fille se réfugierait pour se protéger des houles et remous de l'amour exclusif, disons ravageant avec sa mère."

mother subject to his authority and seductive alternative to the Father's Law, and the family as buffers and milder reminders of social rules. These models support the separation and set limits between bodies. Yolande Govindama (2011) observed how maternal hatred can expose the daughter to abuse and incest by the father. In this context, she demonstrated how culture is protective of these abuses, by fixing the maternal and paternal functions in the generational order.

The daughter can be left to face a ravaging relationship with her mother when the father does not occupy his function. At this point, culture determining the mother as primarily responsible for her daughter's education can be a factor that favors a bond of control and makes it more difficult for the daughter to resolve this *ravage*.

What is expected for this resolution is that the fascinating, dazzling, and persecuting image of the female body of enjoyment is reached to the point of decay (Lessana, 2000, p. 12). At this moment, according to Lessana, and only there, the exit of the *ravage* will be effective, and will leave a scar on each of the two bodies. In our previous publication in this collection, we discussed how women are depicted in contemporary African literature. We used the story of Bertha and Megrita (*La négresse rousse*, Calixthe Beyala, 1997) as an example. In this section, we can use it to show how adornment plays a role in escaping the *ravage*. In that story, Bertha is a destructive mother, and Megrita her troubled daughter. They share an ambivalent relationship, where Megrita is the witness to her mother's manipulation of men, unable to take a position to defend themselves or her. The arrival of a stranger in the village gives her the window she needs, to find her image and become a woman for herself. She is wildly attracted to this stranger and does not understand why. This paragraph describes how she gets ready to go and see the stranger when she suddenly becomes obsessed with him:

> And I, the girl with red hair, with the thought in the back of my mind that if the shadow of the Stranger persecuted me so much, it was the gods' will and that I had to submit to it, I took a bath, anointed myself with beauty products of my own making. Mango juice mixed with carrot and lemon peel, marinated in honey. This apotheotic mixture, without which, I thought, I would not have been able to become a woman, I let it penetrate

my body, even in my ramifications. I went to the bathroom and, with the help of the small pots of colors, the bottles, the brushes, I shaped the ideal mask of seduction which would allow me to conquer the Stranger.

Satisfied with the image that the mirror hung on the wall reflected to me, I put on a bra, a birthday present from Lady Mom, which I filled with cotton beforehand. I put on a pure wool dress, too warm for the season, but it came from France.[3] (p. 71)

This paragraph represents brilliantly how Bertha's shadow finds an equal match in the Stranger's, clearly representing the Other. He is unlike any other representative Megrita has met before and allows her to imagine a way out of this destructive relationship. In the book, she evokes a love story with a young man from an upper social class. She is hopeful about this as a "legal" destiny; however, given her poverty, this lover dismisses her, leaving her because of her mother's reputation. She tries to find a respectable image and be different than her mother but sees how society has already judged her. The Stranger is the "port" where she goes to take refuge, from the destructive relationship with her mother. Later, when he is revealed to be untrustworthy, she discovers that she is pregnant, and leaves the village to find her real father. Her mother, distraught to have lost her biggest strength (her daughter), loses everything that made her powerful and instead of being the one using men for her satisfaction becomes the one being used and disrespected.

This act of adorning and looking at herself in the mirror is symbolic of her getting out of this *ravage*. The products, dress, and even attitude are a costume, a shield she puts on to meet this Stranger whom she sees as a masculine figure representing the Other she has been waiting for, because every other member of this community was always a reflection of her

[3] Translated from original quote in French: "Et moi, la fille au cheveu rouge, avec en arrière-plan de l'esprit que si l'ombre de l'Étranger me persécutait autant, c'était la volonté des dieux et qu'il fallait m'y soumettre, je pris un bain, m'oignis de produits de beauté de ma fabrication. Du jus de mangue mélangé à un zeste de carotte et de citron, mariné dans du miel. Ce mélange apothéotique, sans lequel, pensais-je, je n'aurais pu devenir femme, je le laissai pénétrer dans mon corps, jusque dans mes ramifications. J'allais dans la salle de bain et, à l'aide des petits pots de couleurs, des flacons, des pinceaux, je façonnai le masque idéal de séduction qui me permettrait de conquérir l'Étranger.

Satisfaite de l'image que me renvoyait le miroir accroché sur le mur, j'enfilai un soutien-gorge, cadeau d'anniversaire de Dame maman, que j'emplis au préalable de coton. Je revêtis une robe pure laine trop chaude pour la saison, mais elle venait de France."

mother. Either they could not see Megrita as different or they submitted to Bertha's powerful position.

This example shows how the *ravage* can be represented in the mother–daughter relationship. We have seen previously in this book how society plays a mediation role and allows identification for the daughter. The author notes that her bra was a birthday present from Lady Mom, ironically the only woman under their roof who is considered and respected. Wearing the bra equals taking her freedom and in the same moment retaining that red thread of her lineage. It is some sort of heritage she keeps from her mother to become a Lady on her own terms. This piece of cloth has the symbolism of a significant heirloom of femininity, and the author underlines the significance of transmission and *ravage*, as Kessaci has shown (2015, p. 100).

Megrita gets pregnant after this relationship with the Stranger, and she decides to break the cycle of violence, because she understands how her mother has suffered from her own mother and what made her so aggressive toward her daughter. By leaving the village and going to find her father, she offers herself and her daughter a fresh start in another environment, where society and ancient hatred will not pollute their life.

Hence, through these theories and story, we have seen how the superego comes from the Maternal Other and remains a strong reference and implicit fearful figure. The feminine Oedipus is largely impacted by the father's and society's presence and actions. They shape the perception of the Other and represent an elsewhere for the girl subject to address her demand and try to fulfill her desire. In the next section, we will define the concept of Masquerade and see how it can be a designed strategy for women, to find their place in the interaction, facing the Other's gaze.

6.1.3 Masquerade as a Strategy

After Joan Riviere introduced the concept of Masquerade, Lacan (1964) rebounded on this concept and defined it as follows:

> The masquerade is not what comes into play in the necessary parade, at the level of animals, for the pairing, and as such the ornament is revealed there,

> generally on the male's side. The masquerade has another meaning in the human domain, it is precisely played at the level, no longer imaginary, but symbolic.[4]

Jean-Michel Vivès (2003) has studied Lacan's conception of masquerade. According to this author, the feminine gender is "nothing" so the woman will construct an appearance that will replace what she "has" and mask the lack. This "nothing" refers to the basic genital status, where the penis is and defines the masculine gender, whereas its absence equals non-existence, until the realization of the desire to have a child. The masquerade can be understood as the organization of an optical illusion. This represents all the characteristics creating an illusion and simultaneously allowing it to be maintained for the masked woman to believe in a true essential femininity in herself, while masking the lack. The feminine masquerade implies the notion of gaze, from the Other. It exceeds his gaze in the fact that it articulates femininity in a specific way. Indeed, when offering herself to the gaze, the girl invites the Other to an encounter and a response.

When the woman constitutes herself as object of the Other's desire, this brings her back to reminiscences of her relation to the Maternal Other, and she faces the abyss of his power. When Vivès underlines the consequences of this gaze and its value for the narcissistic construction, he finds that the feminine subject is attached to her confirmation by the Other, and if she does not obtain it, she doubts. As cited previously, Megrita is very representative of this conception, because she is facing her mother's shadow, in everyone's gaze, and has trouble defining her image. She works on her body to design her appearance and feel dissociated from Bertha. The author's idea of her make-up fabrication emphasizes her construction and preparation to become her own woman. From the beginning of her story, she is fragile and vulnerable. However, this ritual makes her attractive, and people finally see her. Her attraction to the Stranger is the force that drives her to her revelation.

---

[4] Translated from original quote in French: "La mascarade n'est pas ce qui entre en jeu dans la parade nécessaire, au niveau des animaux, à l'appariage, et aussi bien la parure se révèle-t-elle là, généralement du côté du mâle. La mascarade a un autre sens dans le domaine humain, c'est précisément de jouer au niveau, non plus imaginaire, mais symbolique" (p. 193).

Returning to Riviere's theory, the masquerade was in place to hide and disguise her patient's strength, because she has an ambivalent relationship with her father, whom she fantasmatically defeated, when she placed herself in a superior position of knowledge. Hence the masquerade was her overtly feminine behavior, seeking protection from men and acting flirtatiously with them. In this case, body techniques, clothes, adornment, and even womanly ways of speaking can be perceived as parts of this masquerade. And we can imagine that culture supports the masquerade and promotes womanly behaviors in girls and women. Indeed, we have seen how body techniques and personality traits have been encouraged since girls' education.

Moreover, Lacan insists on the lack or emptiness that this masquerade hides, creating a form and arousing interest from an illusion. This means that this abstraction that is called "woman" is dressed and wrapped in femininity, creating something from the lack, and appearing attractive especially because of this lack, through the process of masquerade. Lacan refers to the "parade" describing men's attitude of displaying signs of masculinity, even though they will only gain phallus through their successful interactions.

Other images that are very representative of the masquerade are the characters of Ndjeddo Dewal's seven daughters. They are beautifully dressed and adorned; however, they are illusions and tricks the witch uses to attract young men. They are true representations of femininity as they attract men's gaze, showing marks of seduction, and are technically powerless, but used as weapons by their mother. Because the witch needs her daughters to be powerful, she does not "have" and neither do they. Men are attracted by these girls because they represent femininity and make them show their masculinity, replaying the Lacanian duality masquerade/parade. They start to be anchored in the real word only when the witch is defeated, and then they are no longer dangerous.

We showed this image as represented by the tool Tampsy Optoa[5] to a young man and he gave the following answer:

[5] Tampsy Optoa is a psychosocial projective tool based on African oral tradition and storytelling. It is used for clinical psychotherapy and psychosocial education. More information can be found at the website www.tampsy-optoa.org.

> This image? Well, it makes me think, when a man is with a girl, she lets herself be seduced, maybe when there is too much pleasure, she can control herself, he can't control himself, and the worst, the girl can take advantage of this weakness. That's what I see.
>
> Yes, as we say all the time when … when … when your wife wants you to, you give her something, and she waits for the night to come, she does her tricks, her things and maybe there when you are too excited, she asks you something, you will do it. That's it, you hear it a lot, that's what it makes me think, actually. Because the man let himself be fooled, and the lady took advantage of that to murder him and give his blood to…the witch.

As this patient describes, the daughters are playing the role of vulnerable women, and get men to feel powerful in the interaction. Although they are seducing these girls, they do not realize that the witch is controlling their interactions, and they are not at all in command. The masquerade appears through the daughters' disguise, seductiveness and flirtatiousness. Here, the male patient makes a connection to sexuality, and the fact that men are not in control in this department, even when they think they are. This illusion of control and the attitude of seduction are significant for the concept of masquerade, because women appear to be vulnerable and seduced, and this makes them attractive, especially because of these weaknesses. In this way, they gain men's trust, fooling them into believing that they are only passive subjects.

In this case, the daughters do not have a strategy, as they are only used as weapons, for their mother. However, Megrita does have a strategy in her masquerade: she aims to monopolize the Stranger's gaze and gain strength in her community, as her mother did in her time. Her distant goal is to finally be free of this situation of hostage to her mother's actions. But being driven to him, almost beyond her conscious control, makes her vulnerable because she does not know why she is so obsessed with him and explains this obsession as the "gods' will." To the rest of the community, she looks confident and attractive, while she is powerless in front of the Stranger.

Comparing those images and characters helps to understand both sides because Megrita is a woman character from a female writer and our patient is a man, looking at pictures of a female character in a story. Megrita sees how her attraction to the Stranger is out of her control and wears a costume to be a woman for the occasion. This movement is liberating to her, and she put her best efforts into the realization of this act of seduction. In her position, the Other is her savior and will see her. She is fleeing her mother's shadow, the Maternal Other castrating her, and preventing her from taking her independence.

The seven daughters are seen as destructive, because in our patient's view they incarnate castration anxiety, reminiscent of the Maternal Other, and the masquerade has the goal to lower this vigilance in order to not be perceived as a threat to masculinity. He insists on their tricks, and sexual attractiveness, and generalizes it to every woman and wife. His own castration anxiety appears here and is directed to the Maternal Other. When we imagine this fear as common in men, we can think of masquerade as a strategy for women to avoid their anger and retaliation. Joan Riviere's patient was in that situation where she developed that attitude unconsciously because she felt like she had taken possession of her father's intellectual superiority and had the unconscious fear of castration as a punishment. Her reaction was to fake being in a position of inferiority and look harmless to these men, all representing her father. Her masquerade was directed to the Other because he was the actual depositary of the phallus.

To conclude this section, we can say that masquerade is a set of attitudes women are aided by culture to develop, aiming to hide their resemblance, reminiscence, or connection to the Maternal Other. This masquerade is designed to lower the viewer's castration anxiety and avoid defiance. Eugénie Lemoine-Luccioni (1983) in her research insists on the illusory aspect of masquerade, and the anger it fights:

> And who can say if the display of femininity with which the woman regales the man in this same time is not the simple mask of an unconscious masculinity, that will appear in the following century, in the Americas as in our old Europe? Joan Rivière denounced this mask, almost half a century ago. It means that the woman is afraid to show that this imaginary phallus, she

> could not borrow it from the father, and attributed it to the Mother without quite believing in it: contempt for the man and exaltation of the woman throwing her into the most cruel anguish. The salvation mask is indeed only a fragile screen. What it is necessary to affirm with force, it is that the phallus, the woman does not believe in it. 'It is a swindle; prostitutes know it', could say a Belgian psychoanalyst, Serge André. Well! yes, the phallus is a swindle, like the mask.[6] (1983, p. 33)

Thus, as much as the masquerade is illusory, the parade underlines the evidence that the phallus is equally unsubstantial, and both games are played to trick one another. The author pursues her thinking to prove how illusory the phallus is:

> In fact, if the penis were the phallus, men would not need feathers, ties or medals. They wouldn't need badges. They would not need panache. The parade, just like the masquerade, thus betrays a defect: the phallus, the Bororos would not have invented the penile case to which was reduced, says Lévi-Strauss, their first clothing. The penis becomes phallus only exhibited and hidden at the same time.[7] (1983, p. 33)

Therefore, the masquerade and the parade demonstrate that in the game of power, played by the genders, men and women develop their strategies to fool each other, displaying assets that are socially constructed to incarnate forces and symbolic attributes. Culture plays a large part in this game of power, as it determines the significant value of these

[6] Translated from original quote in French: "Et qui peut dire si l'étalage de féminité dont la femme régale l'homme dans ce même temps n'est pas le simple masque d'une masculinité inconsciente, qui se fera jour au siècle suivant, aux Amériques comme dans notre veille Europe? Ce masque Joan Rivière l'a dénoncé, voilà près d'un demi-siècle déjà. Il signifie que la femme a peur de montrer que ce phallus imaginaire, elle n'a pu l'emprunter au père, et l'a attribué à la Mère sans y croire tout à fait: mépris de l'homme et exaltation de la femme qui la jettent dans l'angoisse la plus cruelle. Le masque salvateur n'est en effet qu'un fragile écran. Ce qu'il faut bien affirmer avec force, c'est que le phallus, la femme n'y croit pas. "C'est une escroquerie; les prostituées le savent", a pu dire un psychanalyste belge, Serge André. Eh bien! oui, le phallus est une escroquerie, comme le masque."

[7] "À vrai dire, si le pénis était le phallus, les hommes n'auraient besoin ni de plumes, ni de cravates, ni de médailles. Ils n'auraient pas besoin d'insignes. Ils n'auraient pas besoin de panache. La parade, tout comme la mascarade, trahit donc un défaut: le phallus, les Bororos n'auraient pas inventé l'étui pénien à quoi se réduisait, nous dit Lévi-Strauss, leur première vêture. Le pénis ne devient phallus qu'exhibé et caché à la fois."

symbolic attributes. Indeed, as much as Culture supports this process, it is supported by history, social representations, politics, and economics, to maintain a seeming balance of power. Women in this game adorn and are encouraged to continue adorning in a specific manner to maintain the masquerade, so this castration anxiety stays at a lower level, and does not empower them enough. Simultaneously, as seen in Boni-Le Goff 's example in the previous chapter, they have managed to put their creativity to work and design styles of adornment that offer a sense of empowerment. In the next chapter, we will see some clinical examples of this strategy.

6.2 Adornment as an Optical Illusion of the Feminine Mystery

Adornment evolves and varies with time, social status, and age. It is highly cultural, but also reflects individual and sub-cultural information. We have discussed how fashion is a field where creativity can be explored, but also how at the individual and sub-group level, people can express their political, religious, and cultural opinions. Women can invest this space to claim their identity, will, and positions. In this section, we will discuss how at the cultural level, femininity can be representative of this masquerade. Indeed, education is highly tinted by sociocultural and religious representations, and thus we will see how these can reinforce the masquerade, using values and stigmas to depreciate behaviors that trigger men's anxiety or challenge their authority. In fact, in the second chapter, we saw how certain personality traits such as impatience, recklessness, and irritability can be highly depreciated, and even considered symptomatic of mental disorders. In contrast, smoothness, grace, patience, and compliance are the best qualities for women, representing feminine ideal and purity. We also saw the connection between women's representation and nature, showing how they are supposed to host men's personalities, and accommodating their needs just like nature is supposed to be nurturing and welcoming.

Masquerade is a reaction to this environment, and a response to this education, while being one of its primary teachings. In this section, we will first discuss what in West African education represents femininity and masquerade. The masquerade we will put in perspective is not solely that of adornment, but the entire womanly behavior as Riviere showed, as a costume of femininity. Secondly, we will see how the veil can be a symbol of this masquerade. And finally, we will discuss women's empowerment, and see how this masquerade can be a vector for them to express their potential and establish a different game of power.

6.2.1 Femininity and Masquerade in Society

Devereux explained how each person is "enculturated" in their environment and adopts certain ways of living and thinking:

> Each individual is 'enculturated' by others urging them to conform to cultural norms. This awareness of the normal individual that culture is something that is first learned and then internalized emerges indirectly from the fact that, after a successful analysis, the patient becomes aware of the extra-psychic origins of his or her superego; this is a common observation in clinical practice. Another characteristic of the normal individual is their capacity to understand and live the culture as a system structuring the man's vital space by defining the 'appropriate' ways of perceiving, evaluating and living the reality, both natural and social. Moreover, culture not only confers meaning and value to the components of this vital space but imposes the way of structuring these components into a meaningful whole. In short, the normal subject manipulates and lives the cultural items according to the meanings and values compatible with the contemporary social reality, on the one hand, and his true status and chronological age on the other hand.
>
> (…) The normal individual is content to recognize the objective reality of the sick society in which he has to live, without blindly introjecting it. He will rather seek to survive long enough to inflect this cultural reality in

the direction of an increased rationality and a greater efficiency on the human level.[8] (Devereux, 1973, p. 97)

We have defined and discussed the concept of superego, and how it is indeed imported from the exterior. In this citation, Devereux confirms how the individual can use inherited manners and codes to adjust to a conflictual situation, and we can see this as a strategy. In the previous section, we have observed how masquerade could be a strategy to face a demanding superego. In this section, we will discuss how women are experiencing this masquerade femininity in different cultural environments.

Culture promotes certain body techniques, rules of education, and body treatments to enhance specific feminine qualities and reduce depreciated tendencies. In the physical dimension, we will address the Wolof concept of *diryànké*, describing a feminine ideal valued in society.

Lamine Ndiaye (2018) has written an important piece about the Wolof massage, and has rightly described how it socializes the body. Indeed, he states that in the Wolof conception, the newborn is not fully determined in terms of gender, and massage as a body technique has the purpose of shaping the body and connecting biological and social identities.

For girls, massage is performed to enhance the hips, strengthen the chest, and accentuate the lower back curve. These specificities aim to facilitate the hip rolling movement in women's walk. As a body technique

[8] Translated from original quote in French: "Chaque individu est 'enculturé' par d'autres qui l'incitent à se conformer aux normes culturelles. Cette conscience qu'a l'individu normal de ce que la culture est quelque chose qui s'apprend d'abord et qui s'intériorise ensuite ressort indirectement du fait qu'à l'issue d'une analyse réussie, le patient prend conscience des origines extra-psychiques de son Sur-Moi; la chose est d'observation courante en pratique clinique. Une autre caractéristique de l'individu normal est sa capacité de comprendre et de vivre la culture comme système qui structure l'espace vital de l'homme en définissant les manières 'appropriées' de percevoir, d'évaluer et de vivre la réalité, tant naturelle que sociale. En outre, la culture non seulement confère signification et valeur aux composantes de cet espace vital, mais impose le mode de structuration de ces composantes en un tout signifiant. En somme, le sujet normal manipule et vit les items culturels en fonction des significations et des valeurs compatibles avec la réalité sociale contemporaine, d'une part, et son statut véritable et son âge chronologique de l'autre.

(…) L'individu normal se contente de reconnaître la réalité objective de la société malade où il faut vivre, sans pour autant l'introjecter aveuglément. il cherchera plutôt à survivre assez longtemps pour infléchir cette réalité culturelle dans le sens d'une rationalité accrue et d'une efficacité plus grande sur le plan humain."

this characterizes the social preference for a slow gait and gracious movements. This gait is representative of the *diryànké* woman conception, representing a beauty ideal of a woman with curves and gracious hip rolling movements. In his paper, Lamine Ndıaye gives his representation of this concept. We will analyze his declaration, and discuss how his masculine position can be put into perspective:

> It is necessary to point out that, in spite of the transformations known by the body, among the Wolof of Senegal, still today, the ideal body morphology is that of the *diryànké*, a corpulent woman letting spread on her passage, the odor of perfumes to the thousand essences of flowers. Nowadays, there is nothing to suggest that the '*diryànké* style' has been devalued. In the Wolof country, still today, the woman seems to blossom by living concretely her femininity if, and only if, she is socially considered as a *diryànké*. This is the body model that it is customary in Wolof society to impose from the very first days after birth. Moreover, the young girl, with her slow and controlled gait, is thought to be a future *diryànké*, even if her clothing habits are of the Western type. This means that the ways of doing and acting of the latter are still valued and will undoubtedly remain so.[9] (2018, p. 272)

Lamine Ndiaye's position transcribes several representations:

- Firstly, that there is a change in society toward a European ideal promoting thinner and Westernized women, but the Wolof society is still attached to its own beauty standards.
- Secondly, the *diryànke* is not only bodily, but also includes coenaesthetic and movement dimensions. Indeed, the author describes a mas-

[9]Translated from original quote in French: "Il faut signaler que, malgré les transformations connues par le corps, chez les Wolof du Sénégal, encore aujourd'hui, la morphologie corporelle idéale est celle de la diryànke, femme grosse qui laisse répandre, sur son passage, l'odeur des parfums aux mille essences de fleurs. De nos jours, rien ne prédispose à penser à une dévalorisation du 'style diryànke'. Dans le Pays wolof, encore aujourd'hui, la femme semble s'épanouir en vivant concrètement sa féminité que si, et seulement si, elle est socialement considérée comme une diryànke. C'est ce modèle de corps qu'il est d'usage, en milieu wolof, d'imposer, dès les premiers jours, après la naissance. D'ailleurs, on pense de la jeune fille, à la démarche lente et contrôlée, même si ses habitudes vestimentaires sont de type occidental, qu'elle est une diryànke en herbe. Les jeunes filles jouent alors à la diryànke, ce qui veut dire que les manières de faire et d'agir de cette dernière sont encore valorisées et le resteront, sans aucun doute" (2018, p. 272).

culine position of erotic feminine representation illustrated by the gait, and fragrance, representing femininity and seduction.
- Thirdly, the author promotes the maintenance of these cultural representations into the next generations. Implicitly, this remark on young women not being able to explore their femininity out of this cultural representation can be perceived as a description and a warning.
- And finally, he dismisses the argument that European clothing would promote Wolof women's acculturation, and notes that the gait makes the difference.

This paper transcribes a masculine position, of the author, and his own representation of the Wolof society and of women's social image. As much as the *diryànké* is a socially valued model, it still represents social expectations of women, and they are supposed to perform and adorn in a certain way to conform. In the previous section, when interviewing stylists, we saw how in the Senegalese society women have various beauty ideals that integrate all body forms, and this is represented in traditional and modern fashion, through fluid clothing enhancing shapes. Women adorn and use fashion to express themselves, as these creators have asserted. However, this representation of the author underlines the *diryànké* concept as a masculine preference that is globally and socially validated as an ideal of femininity. Indeed, the massage reinforces this conception, and operates this transformation on the body to support ritualistic and cultural ideologies, but in the reality of social life, women experience their body as their own.

This erotic representation of the female body also transpires in Monènembo's description of the princess, as cited in Chap. 4:

> Her shoulders were covered with a frail lace shawl which let glimpse her pulpy and firm breasts with the ends surrounded of areolas color of honey and on which came to beat a dense network of necklaces of rush and pearls. Her face with regular features gleamed with copper reflections in the emerging sunlight. From the side, she looked like a child despite her slender height and her rounded breasts. But from her beautiful clove-shaped

eyes came out a look of eagle proper to those who were born to scold and order.[10] (2008, p. 59)

In this fragment of the author's description, we can observe the differences between Wolof and Fulani representations of femininity and beauty. As much as the Wolof culture emphasizes the body's firmness and curves, the Fulani culture is more likely to lay the stress on the fineness of facial features, and skin color. Indeed, the *diryànké* concept is described as proper to the Wolof and highly valued in this context.

Both authors transcribe a masculine position on femininity, promoting either seduction or fragility as determining of beauty. It seems these characteristics are truly representative of the masquerade femininity per se. As psychoanalysts explained in the previous sections, what makes the woman desirable is this fundamental opposition to the man. As massages are performed differently, minds are shaped respectively. In fact, women are designed to be curvy, in opposition to a muscular and firm masculine body. They are described to be fragile and delicate in opposition to men's sturdiness and strength.

As such, women are invited to evolve in this frame, and use these assets, to keep their place in society. When they do not conform to this setting, social judgment can be expressed as dismissive. However, women have found ways to create their own frame, and appropriate their style. Therefore, this masquerade femininity has taken a social dimension, allowing self-expression. If, as Riviere has shown, this masquerade is a psychological construction serving a purpose, in our context it is a social construction, built to ease this anxiety shared in the collective unconscious. It is transmitted socially from one generation to the next to maintain social roles. However, at the gender level, on women's side, it is a socially valued behavior that can help facilitate their navigation in society, without raising fear and aggressiveness. On the individual level, every

[10] Translated from original quote in French: "Ses épaules étaient recouvertes d'un frêle châle de dentelle qui laissait entrevoir ses seins pulpeux et fermes aux bouts cernés d'aréoles couleur de miel et sur lesquels venait battre un réseau dense de colliers de jonc et de perles. Son visage aux traits réguliers luisait avec des reflets de cuivre dans la lumière soleil naissant. De profil, elle avait l'air d'une gamine malgré sa taille élancée et ses seins arrondis. Mais de ses beaux yeux en forme de gousse sortait un regard d'aigle propre à ceux qui sont nés pour gronder et ordonner."

woman has the power to control her effect on others through this masquerade.

In the next section, we will see how the veil, increasingly used in West Africa, is one of the symbols of this masquerade femininity.

6.2.2 Veil of Femininity or Masquerade

According to Eugénie Lemoine-Luccioni (1983): "the clothes offer to see, only to hide, what is showing anyway, which is the desire; not beyond."[11] Thus, we can say with this author that clothing gives substance and allure to this masquerade, supporting the optical illusion. She describes the veil as something that hides but reveals at the same time.

Aline Tauzin (2001), in her research conducted in Mauritania, questions the purpose of the veil for Moorish women. She analyzes the Lacanian concept of lack in the gender dynamic and shows how representative the veil is in this perspective. She generalizes it to the Arabic world, underlining how the veil actually *phallicizes* the female body, making it the object of desire, while showing its jouissance. When covering their body with a veil, women subtract their lacking body from the gaze and anchor the desire, thus being in a position of power. The author discusses the action of seduction behind the veil:

> As for the seduction that she puts into play, hidden behind the veil, it is as devastating as her acts. It is not that of the masquerade, necessary to the emergence of the male desire, prelude to the establishment of a love relation to which it would be the condition. It is a man's capture, putting him in object position. The veil, instead of playing to hide the woman's lack, then becomes curtain, a curtain intended to mask the horror of its jouissance.[12]

---

[11] Translated from original quote in French: "Le vêtement donne à voir, à sa seule fin de le cacher, ce qui de toute façon se montre, à savoir le désir; pas au-delà" (1983, p. 43).

[12] Translated from original quote in French: "Quant à la séduction qu'elle met en œuvre, cachée derrière le voile, elle est aussi dévastatrice que ses actes. Ce n'est pas celle de la mascarade, nécessaire à l'émergence du désir masculin, prélude à l'établissement d'une relation amoureuse dont elle serait la condition. C'est une captation de l'homme, qu'elle met en position d'objet. Le voile, au lieu de jouer à cacher le manque de la femme, devient alors rideau, un rideau destiné à masquer l'horreur de sa jouissance" (2001, p. 83).

This citation shows how unbearable woman's jouissance is to humanity and men specifically. Being confronted with this jouissance, men face their castration anxiety. The veil then appears as a compromise, developed to fake submission, while retaining phallus, on the side of the desired object. Women hide and thus appear to have something to hide. Under their disguise, the shape of an imaginary phallus is developed and fantasized. If, as Lemoine-Luccioni has written, the phallus does not exist and is only fantasized to make sense of genders and genitals, how can we explain this game of power?

It seems that what is at play in every relation to the other gender is our representation of the Other, the Great Other, presiding over our relationship to ourselves, and every other that comes next. Others are mirrors of our own image, emphasizing our differences and aiming to explain them. We always come back to this tumultuous primary relation to the first Other, in her natural aggressiveness and omnipotence, which then becomes socialized and codified as the acceptable Law. Our physical appearance conditions and defines our communication, and social representations, and therefore adornment is substantially significant. The veil that covers the female body not only speaks to the people who are watching, but also to the Great Other as an opposition or a mask for the female castration. When deciding to hide their body, women act on the castration, and give shape to this phallus they are supposed to "not have." They fill this lack by wrapping it under a cover.

Anne Juranville (2004) supports this vision and brings a deeper insight on this topic from another point of view. This author insists on the male perspective toward the veil. Indeed, men's position on this topic touches the key sensitive point of their contact with the "mythical maternal thing." The veil underlines the specificity of the feminine body while actualizing the castration anxiety because it shows how the woman, as she is the object of desire, is castrated. She can only be the object of desire when she is castrated. Thus, the feminine masquerade follows this rule, this game of power, to enact the castration in one another's imaginary.

Anne Juranville (2004) tries to understand this masculine position as follows:

> Conversely, the hatred of desire and the perverse plugging of maternal castration in the imperative of covering the female body with the veil are the effects of the man's denial for this horror of the void: the unbearable castration anxiety under its imaginary aspect can indeed lead to justify the most regressive and the most violent elements of certain diktats. It is then to make a fetish of the veil, by cancelling the difference that characterizes the feminine and refusing to play the card of desire to the profit of a fascination by the woman whom one tries to give existence to through the belief in Mothers' omnipotence. Mothers or whores: one finds the contrasted representations of the feminine carried by the most extremist speeches.[13] (2004, p. 9)

This author allows us to make a connection between the veil as adornment and the ambivalent relationship to women, represented as pure and evil. The veil allows this duplicity, which Lacan evoked as the way women, through this masquerade femininity, activate men's parade, and give shape to the phallus they are supposed to represent. In this movement, they become objects of their desire, recentering the phallus to their gender. The anxiety of Mother's omnipotence appears on both sides, men and women, as destructive because it socially echoes an anti-developmental perspective. Indeed, if mothers were to embrace their omnipotence, they would express their infanticidal impulses and this would be end of life. Tales and mythology have shown how omnipotent mothers are feared and considered as maleficent. The figure of the omnipotent Mother is mythical and must remain so. This castration, gagging their force, and supported by all cultural rites and traditions, serves the purpose of maintaining this imaginary construction of phallus as connected to social domination, even though it is merely the origin and product of desire.

Adornment, whether related to the veil or concerning the entire system of appearance, is still a screen reflecting our representation of the

[13] Inversement, la haine du désir et le colmatage pervers de la castration maternelle dans l'impératif de recouvrement du corps féminin par le voile sont les effets du déni par l'homme de cette horreur du vide: l'insupportable angoisse de la castration sous son aspect imaginaire peut effectivement conduire à justifier les éléments les plus régressifs et les plus violents de certains diktats. C'est faire alors du voile un fétiche en annulant l'écart qui caractérise le féminin et refuser de jouer la carte du désir au profit d'une fascination par La femme qu'on tente de faire exister par la croyance en la toute-puissance des Mères. Mères ou putains: on retrouve alors les représentations contrastées du féminin portées par les discours les plus extrémistes (2004, p. 9).

Other, and its imprint on us. Awa Thiam (2014), in her research on feminine sexuality in Senegal, has pointed out how the dress code has evolved, toward a globalized mix of traditional and modern clothing. She underlined how younger women, earlier keen on more modern clothing, have evolved toward more traditional adornment. Other authors like Penda Mbow, cited earlier, have shown that the veil is now increasingly popular in the younger portions of society. This movement is explained by social, political, and cultural developments, and is widespread in men and women's groups, representing a global radicalization of society.

However, on women's side, we have observed this change in adornment, in individual situations, as representative of a personal position of body appropriation.

In the previous chapter, we have presented Fatou Diop's research (2013), and some of her participants noted that they wore a veil for their protection against the evil eye, bad spirits, and people's jealousy. One of our participants also mentioned this reason for their practice, stating that their religion and veil protected them from these threats. Reasoning in the light of all these authors' theories, we can imagine that the evil here is a projection of the unconscious representation of women's malevolence. This veil as a masquerade not only covers and hides, but also ties this power inside, ensuring that it will not harm anyone, including the woman herself. Others in this perspective are the recipients of people's projections and host their ancient anxiety from the primary relationship. This representation also refers to the connection with the Maternal Other, and the veil takes this symbolic representation as a potential space of becoming, masking their reflection in the mirror, and allowing the desire. The alterity, as introduced previously, is this potential space where creativity is developed and that allows the emergence of language.

This statement leads us to place our argument in opposition to Devereux's conception of women only being objects of exchange between men. Indeed, as women are always referring to the ultimate Maternal Other, in every relationship, we can imagine that men are objects in this dialogue between women, and their reflections. Adornment being codified is a silent language for this exchange cycle and carries implicit symbolism, supporting women's value as signs.

In the next section, we will see how adornment can be a beacon of women's empowerment, and, paradoxically, can be used against them as objects of submission. Then we will discuss how the masquerade is necessarily a technique including language and manners, to navigate in a masculine society without raising fear and aggressiveness.

6.2.3 Masquerade and Women's Empowerment

In the previous sections, we have discussed femininity and adornment, and pointed out how culture was reinforcing a specific image of femininity to entertain this masquerade and avoid the castration anxiety. Then we considered the veil as a symbol of this masquerade and analyzed the sociopolitical and psychological positions on this topic. In this section, we will address the topic of masquerade from the angle of women's empowerment.

In the description of powerful political figures, we have remarked that their adornment is described as pure, approaching them from holiness. We can take as an example the description of Balkis, the Queen of Sheba in the Ethiopian oral literature. In most of the tales (Pérol, 2006), she is described as a beautiful child, in the pure essence of youth. In one of the tales, she is going to fight a terrible dragon and is described as pure and simply dressed, in contrast to the brutal and violent dragon:

> She put on an unadorned white dress, which made her even more beautiful in its simplicity, wore light sandals, and let her hair flow as if for a run in the mountains.[14] (2006, p. 12).

We can imagine that the representation of the female leader is connected to purity because history has proven that people are more likely to accept their ruler if they are emotionally drawn to them, instead of just being loyal to their power. The young woman incarnating virginity and pure beauty seems to be a representative of God's magnificence, whereas

[14] Translated from original quote in French: "Elle revêtit une robe blanche dépourvue d'ornements, qui la faisait plus belle encore dans sa simplicité, chaussa des sandales légères, et laissa flotter ses cheveux comme pour une course dans la montagne" (2006, p. 12).

the powerful destructive and fearful female political figure incarnates castration anxiety and is depreciated, as if she would inevitably lead to chaos. Here we can see how the figure is detached from the authority of the omnipotent mother and connected to the Great Other, viewed as masculine, and therefore more acceptable.

A true example of this representation is that of Sitti 'Alawiyya in Eritrea (Bruzzi, 2018). She was a Sharifa in colonial times and Silvia Bruzzi has studied her clothing and representation in the country through photography and press reviews. Additionally, she compared her representation to those of Eritrean women who were concubines of Italian colonizers and were called "Madames." They incarnated beauty and sensuality, and also personified the colonizers' phantasies of black women.

> If we compare the case of Sittì 'Alawiyya with the portraits of the so-called Eritrean 'Madams'—whose sensual bodies had become a metaphor for the virgin territory to be conquered in circulation at the time—it seems obvious that the dress codes chosen by the Sharifa emphasize an undeniable responsibility, by covering her sexuality. The act of covering herself is a response to the criticisms carried out by the rival male authorities of the same brotherhood who, as we will see in relation to the controversies over one of her photographs, tried to use a discourse on the 'Islamic morality of women' to delegitimize the political authority she enjoyed in the country.
>
> If the 'Madames''s body was an icon of sexualized beauty, an expression of an illegitimate and asymmetrical relationship, a place of interaction and conflict between colonizers and colonized, the Sharifa's body was that of the saint, an untouchable and asexual body, that of a religious as well as political intermediary.[15] (2018, p. 57)

[15] Translated from original quote in French: "Si on compare le cas de Sittì 'Alawiyya avec les portraits desdites 'Madame' érythréennes—dont le corps sensuel était devenu une métaphore du territoire vierge à conquérir circulation à l'époque—, il paraît évident que les codes vestimentaires choisis par la Sharifa mettent en exergue une responsabilité incontestable, en couvrant sa sexualité. L'acte de se couvrir est une réponse aux critiques menées par les autorités masculines rivales de la même confrérie qui, comme nous allons le voir à propos des controverses sur une de ses photographies (doc.3), essayèrent d'utiliser un discours sur la 'moralité islamique des femmes' pour délégitimer l'autorité politique dont elle jouissait dans le pays.

Si le corps des 'Madames' était une icône de la beauté sexualisée, expression d'une relation illégitime et asymétrique, un lieu d'interaction et de conflit entre colons et colonisés, le corps de la Sharifa était celui de la sainte, un corps intouchable et asexué, celui d'un intermédiaire tant religieux que politique" (2018, p. 57).

The author claims that the Sharifa's veil was seen as closer to those of Christian religious women, and this detail obliged the colonizers to respect her as such, forcing them out of this representation of the sexualized African woman open to an asymmetrical relationship with them. Her respectability and legitimacy were called into question, especially by her fellow Muslim men, who were showing resistance to accepting a female leader. Bruzzi emphasized the differentiation between the Sharifa and regular Eritrean women considered as available to Italians. Indeed, it seemed that this ambivalence between the two types of women was necessary to integrate a relationship of respect between the colonizers and the female leader. This brings us to approach the topic of women's empowerment, and our question is how adornment contributes to legitimating women in positions of power.

In this study on adornment and masquerade, we have discussed the topic of domination, and games of power. Although women have their role in the social world, society still expects them to represent a certain image, and conveys it through education and social values. This ambivalence, represented at many levels of society, between motherhood and femininity, behind the figures of the pure saint woman and the provocative and attractive one, is reflected by adornment. Indeed, the examples cited above show how the figure of motherhood is utterly respected, whereas the figure of femininity is feared or depreciated. Our previous publication on the topic of the devouring mother has studied extensively this figure and her construction. Moreover, in the previous chapters we have seen how rites of passage and body techniques accentuate women's inclination toward a more familial and social role of transmission, criticizing movements of emancipation as marginal and isolating. We have also discussed alterity, and how the Maternal Other, then developed into the figure of the Great Other, contributes to structuring the representation of self through the Ego-Skin concept at the center of the kinesthetic experience.

In this section we can conclude that women find a way to use adornment to change or establish a game of power with the Other. This power can be manifested through seduction, whether this is as a woman or as a mother. We have seen earlier that the figure of Mamy Wata is connected to illusory beauty, jewelry, and wealth, and as a figure of a devouring mother, she incarnates the fantasy of easy promiscuous relationships and pleasure. In this perspective, the character of the benevolent mother is described as the simplest unadorned woman living on the smallest expense. Thus, this opposition emphasizes the rejection and depreciation of emancipated women, considering them as usurpers.

Riviere's clinical case has taught us that this woman, in a position of power in terms of knowledge, needed to be reassured as much as a bomb must be defused. In her phantasy, the male auditorium had to believe in her womanliness, to be reassured themselves, and not retaliate for that knowledge she felt like she had stolen. When reporting this frame of analysis in our field, we can imagine that women, in the African context, in the situation of *diryànkés*, for example, are pushed to perpetuate this style as a masquerade to maintain a sense of peace in men's consideration, or they will be despised as emancipated or acculturated. In this frame, these terms are synonyms for detachment from men's desire. Again extending this reasoning to the thematic of women choosing to wear the veil, we can understand it as a subtraction from men's desire.

Nevertheless, the question of men's desire raises another interrogation: Whose desire are they expressing then? Jacques Lacan has talked about this "Other jouissance," accessed when the woman subject goes beyond the mirror and finds her own image. This masquerade might be representative and constitutive of this jouissance, as it reveals the female body as an elsewhere, incompletely accessible to the masculine diktat of desire.

As much as the Great Other remains the rightful figure of authority, the Maternal Other survives the cultural castration and remains in the unconscious as representative of our archaic premises. Women are always echoing this image, and thus they relay this castration in men's fantasies. This translates into a global social fear of women's empowerment, and general ideas of empowered women's depreciation. Proof of this are ideas of acculturation and lack of transmission connected to the concept of emancipation. Indeed, even in matriarchal societies, women are subjected to men for their representation and are socially validated when they are in a relationship. With the exception of some cultures, the representation of a good woman is often connected to her ability to stay in a long-term relationship, no matter the emotional cost. In contrast, men are validated when they have proven to be able to subject a woman to their desire, and the more they have, the more they appear to be powerful. This is the game of masquerade and parade, ambivalent mechanisms playing the game of power.

In the next chapter, we will analyze some clinical examples, and show how masquerade is represented for each of these women.

References

Abensour, L. (2011). L'ombre du maternel : Extraits réunis par Josette Garon. *Revue Française de Psychanalyse, 75*, 1297–1335. https://doi.org/10.3917/rfp.755.1297

Bâ, A. H. (2004). *Contes initiatiques peuls.* Pocket.

Beyala, C. (1997). *La négresse rousse*, J'ai Lu.

Bruzzi, S. (2018). 1. Femmes, images et pouvoir en contexte colonial. Le cas de l'Érythrée dans l'entre-deux-guerres in Gomez-Perez, M (dir.), *Femmes d'Afrique et émancipation, entre normes sociales contraignantes et nouveaux possibles.* Karthala.

Choukroun, J. (2014). Traitements du corps, subsistance et désubjectivation: Femmes et écritures du ravage. *Recherches en Psychanalyse, 18*, 150–159. https://doi.org/10.3917/rep.018.0150

Devereux, G. (1973). *Essai d'ethnopsychiatrie générale.* Gallimard.

Dor, J. (1985). *Introduction à la lecture de Lacan : La structure du sujet.* Denoël.

Govindama, Y. (2011). Haine maternelle et inceste père-fille. *Figures de la psychanalyse, 22*, 113–126. https://doi.org/10.3917/fp.022.0113

Juranville, A. (2004). Voile, féminin et inconscient. *Adolescence, 223*, 523–532. https://doi.org/10.3917/ado.049.0523

Kessaci, L. (2015). Les deux mères : Figures antagonistes et "ravageantes" de la mère. *Recherches en Psychanalyse, 20*, 133–139. https://doi.org/10.3917/rep.020.0133

Lacan, J. (1958). La signification du phallus. Écrits, Paris, Seuil, coll. Champ Freudien, 1966 (p. 690).

Lacan, J. (1964). Le Séminaire Livre XI, *Les quatre concepts fondamentaux de la psychanalyse*. Paris, Le Seuil, 1973 (p. 176).

Lacan, J. (1974). *Le Séminaire*, livre XXII (1973–1974), séance du 19 février 1974, inédit.

Lemoine-Luccioni, E. (1983). *La robe, Essai psychanalytique sur le vêtement.* Éditions du Seuil, Paris.

Lessana, M.-M. (2000). *Entre mère et fille : un ravage*. Fayard.
Millot, C. (1984). Le surmoi féminin. *Ornicar ? Revue du champ freudien, 29*, avril-juin, 111–124.
Monénembo, T. (2008). Le roi de *Kahel*. Éditions du Seuil.
Ndiaye, L. (2018). Corps du nouveau-né et techniques corporelles chez les Wolof du Sénégal – le massage (damp). *Corps, 16*, 267–274. https://doi.org/10.3917/corp1.016.0267
Pérol, H. (2006). *Contes et légendes d'Éthiopie*. L'Harmattan.
Sachs, H. (1984). Sur un motif de la formation du surmoi féminin, traduit par D. Sylvestre & M. Turnheim, *Ornicar ? Revue du champ freudien*, n°29, avril-juin, 98–110.
Schaeffer, J. (2015). La nuit des Mères Ombre de l'homosexualité féminine. *Revue Française de Psychanalyse, 79*, 735–748. https://doi.org/10.3917/rfp.793.0735
Tauzin, A. (2001). *Figures du féminin dans la société maure* (Mauritanie), Karthala.
Vivès, J. (2003). La vocation du féminin. *Cliniques méditerranéennes, 68*, 193–205. https://doi.org/10.3917/cm.068.0193

7

Theoretical-Clinical Articulation and Analysis

In this chapter, we will present some clinical cases to illustrate this study. These patients were participants in our research, conducted as a clinical psychologist, on the topic of "Hysterectomy, mastectomy, and women status in Senegal" (Diop, 2012). The goal of this research was to understand the implication of these surgical interventions, for femininity and maternity. However, it has revealed that adornment served a specific purpose for these women. In their stories, we will talk about how their appearance was affected and the signification of these changes for them.

The experience of these operations, while emphasizing death anxiety, and showing the representation of the illness, does echo the concept of lack in femininity that we have described in the previous chapter. Although, the topic in question in this book is not the impact of these interventions, we have chosen to use these examples because they are significant to explain and illustrate the concept of masquerade in femininity. These women who have experienced these situations have been through psychological reconstruction, and this process has involved a change in their adornment. To represent the lack described in the previous chapter, using the example of these women is demonstrative, because the loss is reviving this lack, and forcing this reconstruction process.

I. S. Diop, *Adornment, Masquerade and African Femininity*, Pan-African Psychologies,
https://doi.org/10.1007/978-3-031-28748-0_7

These women who have agreed to participate in our research have a story to tell about how they survived this difficult experience, and what their aesthetic and clothing are masking. Their narcissistic reinvestment based on their adornment shows how this masquerade is connected to the Other and society. We will note that this process of narcissistic reinvestment is not to be understood as pathological, but rather as a positive constructive mechanism aiming to build self-esteem and regain self-confidence.

7.1 Methodology and Ethics

7.1.1 Methodology

a. *Questionnaires and Interviews*

For this research conducted in recent years, in Senegal, we interviewed several women one week and then a year after their surgical intervention. The clinical content that we will analyze here is the comparison between the two interviews, to observe how they have evolved during this postoperative year. The interviews that we conducted were semi-directive, because we had a questionnaire ready, to open the dialogue on the following topics:

- History
- Body and health
- Spirituality
- Family and emotional situation
- Sexuality, femininity, and aesthetic
- Maternity, desire for a child, and menopause
- Pain, illness, and death

We started with open-ended questions, to facilitate the dialogue through participants' free associations. Each interview lasted approximately one hour.

b. *Participant Recruitment*

Our sample consisted of eight women, five who had undergone hysterectomy and three who had undergone mastectomy. The sample also included two other women, one who had a hysterectomy and one who had a mastectomy, but their data have been set aside because, unlike the other women in our sample, these women had undergone female circumcision, which we defined as an exclusion criterion, because we couldn't evaluate the impact of this procedure on body image.

All of these women are Senegalese, grew up in Senegal, and underwent their medical treatment at the same clinic and with the same doctor. For this chapter, we will present the speech analysis of two women among our participants, because we found them to be representative of our problematic.

The recruitment process will be detailed in the next section.

c. *Goal of the Research*

In the perspective of doing action-research, our goal was to allow those women to have their voices heard. They are actors of the research, and not passive subjects, being interrogated, to feed us information. They actively participated in the creation of a booklet for future patients, to gather information of their choice, for optimal care. Indeed, the medical environment does not always allow patients to speak out and express themselves, to share their experiences. Women facing such situations are specifically affected, in an intersectional way, because they are subjected to the doctor's judgment, to society's code, and to their husband's will. Their experience as living beings, owners of their bodies, and primarily affected is singular. Conducting this experience allows us to explore their coping and adaptation mechanisms, to see how they manage to navigate this situation and continue to evolve as women, in their specific environments. In the analysis we will emphasize their evolution and psychic movements, instead of pointing out their suffering or victimizing them. This research can be associated to the field of decolonial intersectional feminist psychology.

7.1.2 Ethics

Given the seriousness of the subject matter of this study, the content of the interviews was reported anonymously to protect participants' identities. The interview recordings were also protected for the same reason.

All participants in this study were enrolled voluntarily, with full knowledge of the use of their data for this research. Before each interview, the surgeon explained to each woman the reason for the interview and that there was no obligation to participate. The recruitment protocol was as follows:

1. The surgeon briefly told them about the importance of the research and the presence of a psychologist at the institution who was doing this type of work. He emphasized the limits of his work as a doctor, and the need for psychological research to advance in the treatment of these pathologies. Then he mentioned our research, specifying that if they agreed to participate in it, he would put us in touch for this interview, which he specified would be free of charge for them.
2. If and when the person agreed to participate in this study, we would introduce ourselves to them, alone, after their interview with the doctor and explain again the purpose of this research and that they could still choose not to participate. In this way, we ensured that they would feel free to make their decision in case the doctor's request had been perceived as an obligation.

We made the request in the following manner (in French or in Wolof):

> Hello Madam, I am Ismahan Soukeyna Diop. I am a psychologist here at the clinic. I work with Dr X.[1] Thank you for agreeing to participate in this research, which concerns women like you who have undergone this type of operation, such as removal of the uterus or the breast. We know that it is a delicate operation, and we want to better understand this situation, to improve the follow-up that we offer you. That is why I am asking you to do this interview now. It will last about an hour. We can do it right away if you agree, and then we will meet again next year, if you are available, to see how

[1] The surgeon will be called Dr X.

you feel. Otherwise, you can take some time to think about it, and if you choose to come back later to do it, we can make an appointment for another time.

For all the initial interviews, when people agreed, we conducted them right away. However, when people preferred to call back later, we could see that this meant a refusal, as no callbacks were recorded during this study.

All interviews were recorded with the participants' prior consent, after explaining to them that their data would be completely anonymous and used for clinical research.

All the people in this sample were recruited for this study and met us for the first time on this occasion. In this way, we were able to control for any bias that a previous encounter or relationship preexisting the research might have caused.

7.1.3 Transference and Countertransference Mechanisms

We observed four types of transference mechanisms with the subjects of this research. In the relationships we had with these subjects before, during, and after the interviews, they positioned themselves in different ways with respect to us, according to the representations that we awakened in them.

- The first type of transference is that of the filial relationship, where the participant has put herself in the position of a parent toward us.
- In the second type of relationship, the participant viewed us as another woman, toward whom she had feelings of either rivalry or friendship.
- In the third type of relationship, the participant felt that we belonged to the medical profession and maintained a certain distance due to suspicion.
- Finally, in the last type of relationship, we were perceived as a member of the society and culture to which they belonged. In this framework, we observed feelings of aggressiveness in relation to the fact that they

felt judged, and a need for conformity, in which the participant made sure to adhere to our point of view.

We have reacted to these transference mechanisms accordingly and developed a strategy to prevent our ideas from influencing our participants.

7.2 Clinical Illustrations and Theoretical-Clinical Interpretation

7.2.1 Mrs A

a. *History*

Mrs A. is 43 years old at the time of the interview. She is married and has six children. Her husband often travels for work, and she has moved from one country to another a few times, due to his occupation. Mrs A. was very young when she got married; she had just graduated from college. She wanted to pursue her studies in medical sciences, but her husband advised her otherwise because he thought that a career in this field would not be compatible with married life due to late working hours.

A year before the operation, Mrs A. experienced intense pain after intercourse, and this had sometimes caused her to be admitted to hospital emergency services. Further examination determined a significant lesion in the uterus, and Dr X. advised her to undergo hysterectomy, to avoid severe development. She has struggled to accept this advice, but the pain she was suffering was intense and she was afraid of developing cervical cancer. Years ago, an aunt of hers had died from this type of cancer. The diagnosis was made too late and there was very little chance to save her, so the doctors along with her family did not tell her the truth about her illness. Because of this experience, Mrs A. is very suspicious toward the medical staff, and in the first interview, she is worried that I might have been sent by her doctor to announce bad news. This suspicion fades after a year, and during the second interview, she is relieved and more confident.

b. *Body and Health*

Mrs A. gives precise indications of her symptoms ("lower abdomen, left side," "ovarian problems," "uterus, ovules, tubes"), and she seems to pay a lot of attention to the medical nomenclature of her symptoms ("lesion on the cervix," "ovarian cysts," "sickle cell disease"). She also names medical procedures precisely ("colposcopy," "laser LEEP," "biopsy," "puncture"). This use of medical language may be justified by the fact that Mrs A. refers to her desire to study and work in the medical world when she was young. We also see these medical details as a habit she has built when addressing the medical staff, because in these interactions she is more a body than a person. Her speech is more centered on her physical symptoms than on her feelings. This changes during our second encounter, because some time has passed after the operation, and she has reinvested in her body. We can see here how the Ego-Skin is disrupted by this operation, leaving Mrs A. with an unstable representation of herself. Her speech, centered on the bodily experience, is detached from her feelings as a woman, because she has experienced the medical pathway as dehumanizing.

Mrs A. expresses in the first interview the feeling that she misses a body part, when she says "internally, you're going to say: something... was taken away from me, that you can't explain"; then again in the second interview, through her questioning about the consequences of the operation, "can't what I took away there have consequences?" after she mentions the recurring "hot flashes" since the operation. Mrs A. is hypervigilant about her symptoms and expects her fears to come true; therefore she seizes every symptom as proof of hidden information.

During the second interview, Mrs A. evokes the idea of a change in the body perception: she mentions a "shrinking in the vagina" that she felt during sexual intercourse. It seems that the symptoms that have caused the intervention remain present, and this was a reason for her to avoid sexual intercourse, as she was afraid that the wound was not completely healed after a year and that sexual intercourse could reopen it. At that time, she prioritizes her health above everything and insists on this point as a significant change in her perception of her relationship with her husband.

Mrs A. recalls a conversation between the doctor and her husband about her, and it seems like she is the subject of this conversation without being an interlocutor. Indeed, after the first postoperative check, the doctor told her husband: "Now I have given you a brand new car, so you should be careful." Mrs A. explains that she is glad that the doctor said this and sees it as a warning for her husband. However, she is the primary *driver of this car*, but this is not reflected in their conversation. Refusing sexual intercourse is an act of appropriation of her body. Additionally, this reference to her body as a brand new car is declared with an authentic smile, as if she hears that phrase as a compliment to herself. I believe that this phrase could be interpreted at two levels:

1. It is a reference to her body as an aesthetic envelope, as beautiful as a *brand new car*. And Mrs A. accepts it as renarcissizing compliment.
2. It is a reference to her body as a vessel, a machine that her husband uses to satisfy his desire, and here Mrs A. is glad that the male doctor intervenes as a figure of authority, declaring the boundaries. He appears as a reference to the Other, in front of her husband, stating that he has given him the right to be intimate with his wife, but remains as a surveyor. Thus Mrs A. has the support of her doctor to reject intimate offers.
3. Dr X. elevates himself to the status of a powerful entity, capable of renewing Mrs A.'s body and "giving" her to her husband, as a father would give his daughter in marriage. She accepts him as a tutor and sees him as an ally against her husband.

This declaration by Dr X. could be rightfully seen as dehumanizing, misogynistic, and objectifying. However, one could also think that he is implying a castration threat but uses cultural tricks to state it without overtly frustrating the husband.

Nevertheless, this aesthetic reference to the *brand new car* and its narcissistic validation effect is to be noted.

c. *Spirituality*

The practice of the Muslim religion is mentioned in the first interview, and confirmed in the second, with the trip to Mecca and the wearing of the headscarf. This increase in religious practice in the year following the operation is of interest to us because it can be interpreted as a consequence of the operation, a means of dealing with a certain amount of guilt related to the causes of the illness. The spiritual guide, mentioned twice, seems to have great importance in the decisions Mrs A. makes ("he knows everything"), and appears as a confidant, a religious guide for the family. This conception appears in a different way during the second interview, where the religious attitude is felt less as linked to guilt, and more as a life choice, or a coping strategy. There is also the proud manifestation of a position of religious knowledge, which she now seems to have earned. She has worked throughout the year to gain this religious knowledge and has completed the pilgrimage to acquire the status of *Hadja*. This investment in religion as a field of accomplishment is an effective coping strategy because she grows narcissistically and acquires a better position and others' admiration. Here she becomes more than a woman. Her headscarf testifies to this and is worn like a crown. Here we see how adornment can be a space of narcissistic reinvestment, and symbolically elevate the woman to the status of the saint mother, inaccessible to the lack. With this additional piece, and its symbolic representation, she becomes whole again. Further in this analysis, we will see how this headscarf, masking and filling the lack, makes her phallic and changes her desire.

The idea of divine will and that the disease is caused by God is also expressed, especially in allusions to "Amine," where she thanks God for the positive results of her medical tests, or "man proposes, God disposes" and "God has decided like this." At this point it is not only the illness that is caused by God, but also the fact of having a professional occupation, or not. There is a certain fatality in the events evoked, paradoxically to a clearly expressed awareness by Mrs A. of taking her life in hand, building a new image of herself.

Animism and mysticism are also evoked as a threat and possible cause of the illness. Mrs A. mentions the idea that it could be seen as a cause of her illness, by others, if she was in a polygamous marriage (the work of competing co-wives). By stating that this is not the case for her, she negates this threat, but the fact that she mentions it shows that this idea is present in her mind. Through this allusion, Mrs A. evokes the gaze of others as castrating and threatening. Indeed, they could be envious and jealous, and this illness could be their doing. Recalling our previous chapters, we could say that this operation, experienced as a castration in her reality, and society are representative of a castrating omnipotent Maternal Superego. Against this powerful Maternal Other, she turns to God, as a protector.

d. *Family and Couple Relationship*

Mrs A. was married young and quickly had her children. She had to give up her ambition to work in the medical field, even though it seemed to be what she really wanted to do. Her daughter, with whom she is very close, also has this ambition, and she encourages her to go in this direction.

In the first interview, she does not dwell on her relationship with her husband, except when she brings up the subject of sexuality. But in the second interview, Mrs A. talks a lot about her life as a married woman, and the difficulties she has in communicating with her husband, especially in relation to a conflict over the issue of work and financial independence. She seems to have made the decision to work and become more financially independent. Despite her husband's refusal and lack of means, she chooses to continue in this direction and forces him to accept her decision. It seems like she is trying to regain an image of herself that she had before, when she was more active professionally. She speaks proudly about her education, and the experience and the reputation she had in her former business.

Regarding her family, Mrs A. only talks about her brothers (from the same mother and father), especially the one with whom she is most often in contact, as well as her sister (from the same father) who died of cancer a year earlier. She mentions her mother's death, without saying anything more about what caused it, or the relationship she had with her. During the second interview, the family is presented more in terms of the burdens and responsibilities they represent. When she talks about the various family disputes in which she intervenes, her position as a mediator seems to come with more challenges than benefits, and she does not seem to be acknowledged in return. She expresses her will to be removed of their interactions and focus on herself.

The youngest sisters (of the same father) have given her the title of big sister, to preside over their monthly meeting. This position, acquired upon her return from Mecca, confirms the change in status brought about by this psychic reorganization. She is proud to accept this title, as it also shows respect for her experience as a woman, and her knowledge of spirituality. She adopts a similar posture toward new patients at the doctor's office, to whom she is glad to provide support and guidance.

e. *Sexuality, Femininity, and Aesthetic*

In both the first and second interviews, Mrs A. expresses the will to talk about her sexuality. We understand this wish as the first occasion when she can talk about this topic, with a woman in her care pathway. Indeed, she has had the opportunity to discuss medical symptoms related to this field with the doctor but has not been able to discuss her feelings, her intimacy, and her desire. In the first interview, Mrs A. recalls a painful experience, at a time when she was extremely worried about her health. The doctor's metaphor for her husband and the way she laughs about it show that she may think that this health concern, as well as the previous painful experience, is due to her husband's sexual ardor. The six-month delay before the next intercourse seems to be a solution to postpone the next intercourse.

During the second interview, Mrs A. briefly mentions the changes in her sex life caused by the operation, without being asked the question directly, as if she was waiting to talk about it. She mentions a "shrinking in the vagina," causing pain during sexual intercourse, as well as pain due to a "wound," as if the healing of the operation was not fully complete. We can see here how the traces of the operation remain vivid, despite the time that has passed.

When it comes to offering advice to women who, like her, will go through this experience, Mrs A. dwells on the effects on her sexual life, more than on any other, as the major consequence, and that she had not been sufficiently prepared to face this. The change in sexual relations is mentioned in terms of the profound changes it brings to the couple, and to her in particular. Indeed, Mrs A. presents a change in her relationship with her husband, where she has more expectations from him than before. She speaks of an awareness whereby she has realized that he will not make the same efforts for her that she has made for him, even if she specifies later that he understands the precautions to be taken during intercourse because of her convalescence. We can think that she does not feel supported by her husband as much as she would like to on this point. On the one hand, this is due to his absence for his profession, and on the other hand the fact that he does not support the idea that she has a professional activity herself that could allow her to feel more emancipated. After this experience, she demands this emancipation to gain independence, and no longer accepts his objections.

Femininity is directly addressed in the second interview, when Mrs A. specifies that she would like to be more financially independent, to buy things herself, and "to dress properly." The aesthetic change is emphasized with the wearing of a headscarf. This change is accompanied by a modification in Mrs A.'s clothing style ("apart from the scarf, there are the jeans that I stopped wearing, and for the tops, I wear them up to the knees, at the hips"). Mrs A. is very coquettish in both the first and second interviews (make-up applied, scarf chosen in accordance with the style of dress, and elegant outfit). She was 44 years old during the second interview, which is a relatively young age for a woman who has made the pilgrimage to Mecca. Even though she specifies that she chose to go at a younger age, to be in better shape for the trip, we retain the idea of a desire to change her status. This change seems to be supported by her husband, who offered her this trip.

f. *Maternity, Desire for a Child, and Menopause*

During the first interview, Mrs A. mentions her regret of not being able to give birth to another child as she wished. Although she is the mother of two boys and four girls, she specifies that she would have liked to have another boy, to name him after her spiritual guide. The operation has definitely compromised this aim. She renounces this desire for a child, and her husband seems to support her in this sense, emphasizing the righteousness of their decision, and the priority of her health. This spiritual guide is the family's confidant and plays an important role. During the second interview, she does not express further regrets on this point, but rather talks about the relationship she has with her eldest daughter, to whom she confides a great deal.

The symptoms of menopause seem to be disturbing for Mrs A., both because they are unpleasant and because she did not seem to be prepared for them. Hot flashes are a problem in her daily life and are experienced as disruptive, appearing when she is upset. Mrs A. herself links this increased sensitivity to the appearance of hot flashes at every contradiction and sees these as consequences of the hysterectomy she underwent.

When asked what a woman who has had a hysterectomy should prepare for, Mrs A. does not fail to mention early menopause and not being able to have children as the main consequences. These, along with the difference in sexual life, seem to be the major consequences of her hysterectomy for Mrs A., the ones that really caused a change in her life as a woman. We see here the close link between her identity as a woman and the loss of fertility. Adornment serves the purpose of redefining the lines of her body, and the masquerade is played in the layers of her clothing. From her status as explicitly lacking, after this operation, she covers her body and acts as if she is hiding and subtracting something from the field of sexual exchange. What is this something if not the "nothing" that was left by the operation? Indeed, menopause makes it clear that she will never experience this "something" again, and her reaction of overinvesting in her relationship with her daughter is significative of this change. In this relationship, she is transmitting her heritage as a woman, and encouraging her daughter to seek emancipation. There, in this heritage she transmits, and this knowledge she gathers, she is creating a substance, "something" that makes her whole again.

g. *Pain, Illness, and Death*

Mrs A. mentions several times the pain felt both before the operation, through the symptoms that caused it, and after the operation, with the consequences on sexual life. She explains in detail the painful sensations she had at these two moments ("lower abdominal pain," "too strong, as if I had a cramp," "it feels like there is a wound"), and the elements that accompanied this pain, testifying to the presence of a disease ("blackish blood" during menstruation). The pain felt during sexual intercourse is attenuated by the pharmaceutical product that Mrs A. uses, but her husband's professional routine (being out of town very often) is described as useful, paradoxically to the fact that she evokes a lack of attention on his part, regarding her ambitions of business. This claim translates her will to be no longer seen as a wife, but more like a partner, whom he would trust for a business project.

Illness, and in particular cancer, is a source of anxiety for Mrs A. She clearly describes her fear of this illness and has difficulty voicing the word "cancer." Her difficulty in integrating the idea that cancer is part of her life, through the experience of her late sister, and the fact that, despite this experience, she continues to admit that she has never heard or seen the disease, show that she has a fear of cancer, and is running away from this reality by all means at her disposal ("I thought I had cancer, I thought it was serious," "when you are told something you have not seen, you have never heard… ").

During this first interview, Mrs. A had just come out of the doctor's appointment, where she had been told her diagnosis, indicating that she did not have cancer, but rather a lesion that had been cured by surgery. Although the news is good for Mrs A., her lack of trust in the health care team and her suspicion about the request for the interview are supported by the anxiety about the disease, which she still believes to be threatening.

This anxiety is less visible during the second interview, because Mrs A. has resumed a normal life, even if she mentions a rise in blood pressure, leading to permanent medication. Cancer is not mentioned as a threat to herself, but only when she tells the story of a woman she knows who is having difficulty coping with her illness. She positions herself as serene and calm in the face of the disease, at this point, while happily pointing out that this risk has been eliminated for her.

Death is mentioned with anxiety in the first interview, associated with cancer. However, it is with humor that she evokes this point, in the second interview, defensively, about the anxiety, always present. Death is evoked at two moments, the first time when it is a question of choosing between the desire for a child and the operation ("if you are dead, you are not going to think about … a child"), and the second time in relation to the choice of going early to Mecca because no one knows when death is going to happen. This recourse to religion can be seen not as a possibility to protect oneself from illness and death, but more like a way to prepare for death, to ensure an afterlife in paradise, in agreement with God's rules. This realization seems to have been precipitated by the evidence of illness, and the threat of death that may come "suddenly" and "at any moment," words she herself uses to describe her feelings about these threats.

Facing illness is difficult because it confronts one with both castration and separation anxieties. Death echoes the "nothingness," the absence, and the reduction of the individual to their own fear of scattering. Mrs A. in her attitude toward religion seeks to be in control of her fate, and gains security in this process. The headscarf is not only a masquerade for society but also for death. She is changing, evolving, to be out of reach of this "nothingness." In this movement she is tricking death and castration. This body, which has failed her, is to be tied, embellished and connected to a protective entity, to be powerful in front of the disease. The process of clothing redraws its limits, and they can no longer be erased by the illness. Adornment in this way is used as a masquerade that phallicizes this body, to be in a position of strength. She is no longer just this body left to be taken by the illness.

h. *Summary of the Analysis of Mrs A.*

The need for emancipation is simultaneous with the narcissistic reinvestment, and Mrs A. has chosen to engage it in three fields:

1. In the religious field, Mrs A. has grown closer to God through an increased practice that makes her feel more protected and in control. Her spiritual guide is an ally in this field, and a referent for the Great Other, standing as a mediator between her and her husband. The principal regret she expresses for the loss of her uterus is that she can no longer have children, and she wanted to have a boy that she would name in his honor, to thank him for his prayers and guidance to her family. This new status confirms her connection with him and elevates her to a higher status. She can no longer have children, but can be a guide for younger women, which actualizes a position of maternal power.

2. In the field of sexuality and in her relationship with her husband, Mrs A. has expressed that she feels changed and more demanding toward him. She no longer agrees to make sacrifices, especially when it comes to her health. Therefore, she only accepts intercourse on her own terms. This position is that of femininity, where she expresses her desires, and no longer cares to be submissive. There she regains a position of control and attracts her husband's desire, while rejecting his intimate offers. She becomes inaccessible and is in control of their relationship.
3. In the field of adornment, she takes control of her image and decides to adopt a new dress code that represents her religious status. This headscarf and the attention attached to her clothing represent a new approach to femininity, where she attracts the gaze of the Other. After this difficult experience, creating a sense of emptiness, generating fear and actualizing castration anxiety, Mrs A. rebuilds herself, and expresses her demands to finally be independent in her life. This investment of the sphere of adornment shows how masquerade is used to create an object of affection for the Other to desire, while subtracting this object of her husband's control. She no longer submits herself to his will, and on the contrary makes her own demands, as if she has decided to give more value to herself than he ever did. Being adorned makes her more interesting to the Other and therefore she is no longer exclusively his. We can see this jouissance gained out of his reach as the other jouissance mentioned in the previous chapters, because she has it for herself, and it no longer depends on his desire.

7.2.2 Mrs M.

a. *History*

Mrs M. is 55 years old at the time of the interview. She has an important career, in a big company where she is valued and respected. She lives in her own house, with some family members she accommodates and supports, especially young nieces, who came to study in the city. Mrs M. was married in her forties, and her husband has died eight years ago. She has attempted to have children during her marriage but has had several miscarriages, despite her physical and financial investment in medical treatment. She has noticed a lump in her breast a year prior to the operation and has shown it to her doctor. The latter did not consider this an emergency, and she had to seek a second opinion, with Dr X, who diagnosed breast cancer. She was advised to quickly undergo mastectomy and chemotherapy, to avoid further development of the disease. At the time of the interview, she was interested in having a breast reconstruction in the near future, because she considered it necessary for her sense of well-being.

b. *Body and Health*

Mrs M. mentions the breast several times, and she clearly evokes the emptiness ("there is a void") caused by its absence. The lack is clearly expressed here and emphasized when she talks about wanting to get a breast prosthesis. In the first interview, Mrs M. talks about an internal prosthesis that she would like to have. The confusion between the breast and a brathat one can fill with cotton supports this idea of lack, assuming the illusion that the breast is still present, but would be somehow deflated, emptied of its contents. In the second interview, Mrs M. tells us that she is willing to fulfill this wish, but the fear that the other breast might be contaminated seems to make her hesitate. At this moment she talks about waiting to know if the other breast is contaminated, to make the prostheses for both breasts. This idea of contamination is present several times during the first interview and is reinforced by the real possibility of this risk, implicitly confirmed by the doctor. It indicates the feeling that the disease could spread to the other breast and empty it of its contents. Her reaction of going forward with the ambition of a second mastectomy puts her in control rather than being surprised again by a return of the disease.

The operation is called "ablation" only once, by Mrs M., and the word operation is used throughout the interview, to designate the mastectomy. This last word is not used or repeated by Mrs M. after we mention it once at the very beginning of the interview. She mentions several times that the other breast could also be removed, and says she is not afraid of this possibility, but expects it, as it seems obvious to her. It seems that Mrs

M. talks about this possibility with insistence, and an impression of lightness, in order to exorcise the fear she has of it.

Some elements of medical vocabulary, regarding the care protocol, are present in the interviews ("bandage," "counting," "mammography," "prostheses," "radiotherapy"). Mrs M. makes several mistakes in confusing medical terms, and sometimes has difficulty recalling the names of these procedures, because she has forgotten them. Paradoxically, she gives exact dates and information about her appointments and medical pathway. This shows a certain difficulty in managing this challenging experience, which we can understand as destructuring. Mrs M., being an administrator in a company, applies her knowledge of organization to her care, but somehow is overwhelmed with all this vocabulary and medical specificities. She focuses on this project of breast reconstruction as a leitmotiv to leave this experience behind her and move forward.

c. *Spirituality*

Mrs M. describes herself as "too religious," a "strong believer," and says she has been to Mecca more than five times.[2] She implies that she will continue to go there every time she has the opportunity. Her faith seems to give her a certain strength ("strong believer," "these are my only weapons"). Mrs M. seems to see the illness as being the result of divine will, but questions are still evident on this point. Indeed, Mrs M. says that she does not believe that she has done anything to deserve this; in this expression there is the idea of incomprehension in front of this situation, whereas she says she respects all the principles of her religion. The last pilgrimage to Mecca was made just after she noticed the symptoms of the disease, but she says she "could not cancel that trip," so she waited until her return to consult. At that time, she put her religion before her health, so it is conceivable that she did not understand the illness, after the sacrifice that was made. She says that she "doesn't believe that the illness is a punishment," and especially that she doesn't believe that she "did something to deserve this," but she seems to doubt this idea by specifying, "but it is God who draws, eh," and therefore He might have something against her.

[2] The exact number of times was mentioned, but we have chosen to be vague to protect the participant's anonymity.

In contrast, this tendency is reversed when she evokes serious situations that she has seen or lived before, making her own situation appear less serious. At this point, she repeatedly says, "thank God, because it could have been worse." We can think that in this way Mrs M. de-dramatizes her situation, to escape the reality and the anguish that the disease represents. These situations, in which she saw other women with more serious breast cancer, could, on the contrary, have made her more anxious about the possible evolution of the disease. However, she says she is reassured because she is not at that point. This way of reassuring herself seems to be characteristic of a denial of reality, associated with the anguish of the disease, and her frustration in front of this injustice from God. This idea is confirmed when she says that "praying has its limits…you can't spend all your time praying." This shows exasperation with the lack of benefit from the sacrifices she has made. God is deaf to her prayers. Religion is invested in a superego function, as a morbid constraint that prevents her from existing with her desire.

Expressions of the type "I put myself in God's hands" are numerous and characterize Mrs M.'s reaction to things that upset her. We note this position in the first interview, facing the unexpected illness, and then in the second, with a colleague who had offended her by talking about her illness to the other members of the company. She shows her bitterness in the second case, and indirectly expresses her wish to see this person lose her job, but instead of saying it directly, she "trusts in God," hoping perhaps to see this wish come true. These people who provoke her anger seem to be scapegoats, onto whom she transfers her anger toward God who has made her sick, and makes her suffer despite all her sacrifices.

References to mysticism and animism are absent from the discourse of Mrs M., who seems to have an exclusively Muslim practice, even though this practice is often associated with animism in Senegal.

God is invested as the powerful Other, who punishes and castrates, and simultaneously he is the protector and guarantor of peace. In her comments, we can see how she has spent her life cherishing her religion and applying every prescription. Now, she is in a moment of questioning the causes of this illness. The parents are infantilized, and she is the family's leader.

d. *Family and Emotional Situation*

Family is evoked as a space where Mrs M. is responsible and has a strong decision-making position ("I am the pillar in the family"). This position seems to have been taken without consideration for the family hierarchy, as Mrs M. says she has two elder siblings, a brother and a sister. There is a certain satisfaction in the way she describes her position, as it seems that she experiences it as a success on the family level. In her relationship with her parents, Mrs M. also describes herself in a supportive position, as she does not want to worry them by telling them about her health condition, as they are elderly and sick themselves. This success on the family level echoes her real professional success, as she has a prestigious job in a big company, ("it's very big"), and compensates for her desire for a child.

Mrs M. lives with her nieces, her older sister's daughters, which is common in Senegal. Her nieces depend on her. After her mastectomy, she gave them her clothes as gifts, "without them knowing what it is." The gift of the clothes is at this point described either as a sacrifice, expecting a benefit in return, or as representing the loss caused by the operation, because she will no longer be able to wear those clothes. They belonged to the woman she was before the mastectomy, and that was unapproved by the Other. Giving them away distracts his attention and lets her find another adornment to change her masquerade. In this new role, she needs to change her strategy and appear more vulnerable. Her clothes were signs of her success and privileges, so this reaction in the sphere of adornment means that she might believe that the Other has disapproved her audacity and provoked the illness as a consequence. In the second interview, Mrs M. talks about her niece who poses a problem for her, because of her moods and her bad temper. This niece is said to be unmarried and unhappy even though she is serious in her relationships and a devout follower of the Muslim religion. We get the impression here that Mrs M. sees herself through this niece, and that her difficulty in supporting her at this time may be due to her self-criticism, in the search for causes to explain her current condition.

Marriage is discussed in the first and second interviews, as a possibility and an ambition for Mrs M. The marriage proposals are there, but the fear of being confronted with a man's gaze, with this new body, is holding her back. Her previous marriage, described as polygamous, was carried out after the age of 40, and Mrs M. did not have the opportunity to have a child. The marriage is indicated as the condition to be in a relationship with a man again, because of Mrs M.'s religious devotion. But the fear of rejection is clearly expressed. The idea of having an operation on the second breast seems like an acceleration, to avoid a return of the cancer and then proceed with the breast reconstruction ("it's simpler even"). At the same time, she expresses the fear of loneliness, already encountered when she was in the hospital, after the operation, as a foretaste of what her life would be like. This fear of loneliness can explain her choice to live surrounded by her nieces.

e. *Others' Representations and Society*

The gaze of others is described through the eyes of a man. Mrs M. suggests that she would not be complete in the eyes of another man, because "they are not familiar with this kind of women." In the second interview, she evokes a scene where her niece has surprised her undressed, and burst into tears seeing her missing breast. Here again the glance of others on her lacking body is experienced as violent and painful. There is the idea that this body would cause disgust, sadness, or rejection from others, and at this moment she insists on the need to wear a prosthesis. This prosthesis could protect her from this confrontation with her own sense of her body and give her a socially acceptable image.

The gaze of others is still described in the second interview, but more focused on the disease, which she experiences as stigmatizing. When she talks about her colleague, with bitterness, and the gaze of the other women at her job, she shows several positions, some experienced as irritating, others as encouraging. In the second interview, when she mentions the company doctor's advice not to tell her colleagues about her illness, Mrs M. seems to agree with this advice, and states that she has noticed changes in the attitude of one of her colleagues, who had already been informed of her condition. The colleague disseminating the information contained in the personal files is strongly criticized in Mrs M.'s speech, but she does not confront her to her face, and "trusts God" to avenge her for this provocation. She does respond indirectly to the woman who came to her to discuss her illness. This conversation, probably in a supportive light, is very badly received by Mrs M., who seems to hear it in a condescending light. This idea of condescension seems to characterize the women's attitudes toward her. The criticisms of gossip and backbiting support this idea, and there is a lack of precision about who this criticism is directed at, and the idea of a generalization.

One of the women is described as supportive of Mrs M. This is her supervisor, a younger woman, who takes a great interest in Mrs M.'s health and establishes a friendly relationship with her when she learns that she is ill. The relationship is described as sincere, and Mrs M. seems to find a lot of benefit in it, but there is little information about this woman, as if the relationship was only directed at Mrs M.

This support is not found with her nieces, or with anyone else in her local family circle, and she mentions that she should talk to her brother, because "there has to be someone to share with." Mrs M. justifies this choice by the fact that her brother is "the most intellectual of the group"; he is the one who is abroad. It seems that the choice is made for this brother because he lives abroad and because he is intellectual, and hence the distance will make this task easier for Mrs M. She will not have to see, in this brother's eyes, pity or any other feeling that could make it more difficult for her to live with this illness. The fact that her colleague/friend has a higher hierarchical status than her own is mentioned several times, as she calls her "my boss." This difference in status, added to the description of the brother as "the most intellectual of the group," tells us that Mrs M. finds it easier to bear the gaze of people she considers to be in a better position than her. She does not want to lose the esteem of the people who are dependent on her, and the disease as well as the removal of the breast are experienced as mutilating, not only on her body but also on her image toward her entourage. We understand her attitude of superiority toward this talkative woman at her job, whom she judges unfit for her task, and recruited "anyhow." This attitude is issued in reaction to this colleague's provocation and to all the women who might judge her. Mrs M made her supervisor aware of her illness, and as a result she was able to obtain her protection and maintain her professional security. Her supervisor is a caring woman who listens to her and helps her preserve what she has left. This intellectual brother is abroad, and thus he is not challenging her local leadership position.

f. *Sexuality, Femininity, and Aesthetic*

Sexuality is clearly mentioned by Mrs M. in the first interview, when she talks about what keeps her from getting married again. The operation is described as a brake on her sexual life, because she reports having doubts that a man would agree to be intimate with a woman who is already "like that" before meeting him, when "there won't be much intimacy in the body." Here she implies that she feels incomplete, and for a man to be attracted to a woman, it is necessary for him to have seen her before, when she was whole. This subject seems to preoccupy her, because she has thought about it for a long time. She had already received marriage proposals, but it seems that the fear of the husband's reaction during sexual intercourse prevents her from taking action. The idea of remarrying and having sex again is brought up in the second interview, and at this point there is a game of doubt and back and forth between putting on a prosthesis or not and being in a relationship again. Mrs M. pushes this choice away, and it seems that there is also a certain fear of entering into a new relationship, because as she states, since her husband's death eight years ago, she "has never even kissed another man." This clarification is made in the sense that Mrs M can still wait, as she has waited for these eight years, but her attitude reveals her apprehension about a new relationship. Religion seems to justify this ambition of marriage because according to Mrs M. "in religion it is recommended to get married."

Femininity and aesthetics are expressed thoroughly, especially in relation to Mrs M's clothing habits, which must change after the operation. There seems to be a regret for her former "very coquettish" appearance ("there are a lot of people who don't recognize me anymore…I used to like to do a lot of aesthetics"), and she wanted to show us pictures of her before, to prove this fact. Mrs M. seems to have changed her clothing habits with the disease, not only in relation to the transparent clothes she can no longer wear, but also to the fact that she has adopted a more sober style of dress. This is perhaps to mourn this lost part of herself, or perhaps rather not to show too much joy and attract the wrath of God, who would make her pay for her bad behavior by making her even more sick. This change in adornment confirms the assumption made previously about diverting the Other's gaze and behaving more discreetly to not attract attention. Her adornment used to reflect her power and this discreet look is also a masquerade.

Aesthetics are much discussed in terms of clothing adjustments, between the office, the clinic, and the home. Mrs M seems to have reorganized her clothing habits to fit her new appearance, and lost some of the benefits of wearing clothes she likes. She recalls sharing these concerns with several other women, whom she had observed during her visits to the clinic, and recalls seeing a woman who had not hidden her scar like the others. This memory seems to have marked Mrs M. and she establishes the difference between this woman and herself, as if she clearly wished to distinguish herself from her, as more feminine and coquettish. She talks about the pleasure she feels when she receives compliments from the medical team about her physical appearance ("Sometimes I come, I put on some eye make-up … one day I came here, I had to go somewhere, I had put black pencil on my eyes, there was C. [the head nurse who is a man] and all of them, who came around me, to compliment me"). This is experienced as narcissizing and encouraging, as C. represents a man's gaze and helps her to maintain her image. Mrs M. seems to attach a great deal of importance to the gaze of the Other, and even to define herself only through this gaze. Moreover, since Mrs M. has attached a lot of importance to her physical appearance and coquetry, it seems like it supported her identity and narcissism. When making this compliment, C. gives her reassurance that she is still there, and can be seen. Making an impression on him visually was filling this "void" she mentioned. The missing breast is just an echo of the "void" where she is, because this change in appearance makes her have to become invisible, paradoxically to all the effort she has always made to be seen and mask this lack.

The headscarf is mentioned several times, as a usual accessory, before the operation, because of her religious practice. She used to wear it as an accessory showing her respectability and religious maturity. However, now it has become a way of covering her body, and making the bandage invisible, but this change seems a bit heavy for her, because it is no longer a chosen accessory, and more of a constraint.

g. *Maternity, Desire for a Child, and Menopause*

Mrs M. does not have children, and she mentions this as a potential primary cause of the disease. She later denies this idea, saying that she has seen women who have already had children with this disease, but it seems that this idea is very present in her mind. The two miscarriages were painful, as Mrs M. notes when discussing these these unsuccessful attempts, and the financial efforts to realize this desire for a child. This is told in a tone of guilt and regret. Mrs M. seems to affirm her femininity rather than motherhood; she wanted to be a woman before being a mother, as if there was a counter-identification with a maternal image.

The presence of her nieces around her seems to make up for the lack of children in a superficial way, and Mrs M. complains more about the lack of male company, and talks about her wish to remarry, to feel less alone.

Menopause is not mentioned. Mrs M. simply answers positively to the question when she is asked if she had experienced menopause before the operation, without saying more. Menopause has intruded into the late marriage and put an end to Mrs M's repeated attempts at pregnancy. In this way, we can think that this menopause was a deception for Mrs M.

h. *Pain, Illness, and Death*

References to pain are rare in Mrs M's comments. The only pain mentioned is before the operation, in the symptoms that drew her attention and prompted her to consult a doctor.

The disease is, on the other hand, omnipresent in her comments, first as a fact present in her life with her entourage, even before the disease, then as a condition she has to live with, for the rest of her life. Her parents are described as sick ("my mother is unwell, my father has high blood pressure"), and her husband, who died a few years earlier, is said to have had a weakness, even though he is described as someone who was rarely sick. The early death of her husband also seems to have shocked Mrs M.; it is described as sudden and incomprehensible, just like her disease. There seems to be guilt on the part of Mrs M. regarding her parents' illness and her husband's death.

The illness is carried as a burden, which she does not understand, because despite all her precautions, it could still happen. Religion and God could not protect her from it, or worse, God might have caused it. This disease seems to upset all of Mrs M.'s religious and social conceptions and infiltrate the different spaces of her life. It makes palpable a certain anguish around death in Mrs M. It is even more worrying and incomprehensible because it is unknown. Indeed, Mrs M. specifies that not no one in her entourage or family has ever had cancer, "neither on the maternal side, nor on the paternal side."

Confidence was regained with Dr X. with whom she describes having a good rapport ("when he comes into your room, when you see him, you are reassured, he comes, he teases you, and all that…"). This contact, in the mode of seduction, is experienced as a renarcissization by Mrs M. The head nurse's compliments give her the same effect of renarcissization experienced through the eyes of a man.

i. *Summary of the Analysis of Mrs M.*

This illness brings to Mrs M. the comprehension and the availability of her close relations. The pain and the difficulty of medical care are experienced as a repayment of this debt of life that she has not been able to honor toward God, even though she has sacrificed herself in religious practice. She sees this punishment as an injustice, because she did her best to be a mother, but her efforts were insufficient. This illness shows that the sacrifice of herself, made through the overinvestment of religion, is insufficient, and that she must also sacrifice her femininity, through a search for austerity both in clothing and in her behavior. The gift of clothing is symbolic of this sacrifice of femininity. It also symbolizes a change of adornment, to support her psychological reconstruction, by changing her masquerade.

Her family and her mother in particular are also a source of guilt because she sacrifices herself to them, by putting aside her emotional and social life, to spend all of her time with them. The position that she seems to have in her family testifies to an overinvestment on the part of her parents. By overinvesting in her, her parents have granted her an imaginary power, an illusory phallus. The masquerade lies in that coquetry and search for attention. Her former adornment perfectly represented it, as she appears to be attractive and seductive. The symbolic act of giving her clothes and dressing more discreetly is a coping mechanism, a new masquerade built to distract this maternal superego.

The guilt originates in this place that she thinks her parents gave her at the beginning, that of femininity, and not of maternity. The late marriage motivated by her parents has collided with Mrs M.'s psychic resistances. She experiences the two aborted pregnancy attempts as a refusal of her entry into motherhood. The breast refers to the mother, the maternal that castrates her, and the operation refers to the reality of this castration, by the maternal on the feminine. The body becomes language to express the conflict between maternity and femininity in Mrs M.

The fact that her mother is ill increases the weight of her guilt, because it is also the price to pay for the debt she has not been able to honor. By spending time with her and being in a position of emotional dependence on her, Mrs M. tries to become a substitute for the grandchild she has failed to give her.

She mentions religion as a reason to find an emotional life again, by remarrying. This wish opposes the social image of the woman to which she no longer corresponds, this image that a maternal superego sends back to her, as an ideal. This lost breast represents a narcissistic loss, castration, and the mark of her incompetence as a woman to transmit life. We see here that through God, there is a parental superego; the prayer and the sacrifice serve these parental imagoes. The situation of remarriage is lived as a revival of narcissism, a search for satisfaction, and the use of the pretext of the missing breast prostheses shows the fear of transgressing, feigning, disagreeing, or choosing a destiny different from the one imposed on her by this maternal superego, by devoting herself and by reconstructing a breast after this castration. The threat of losing the second breast comes as a warning in case Mrs M. tries to rebuild her life anyway. This is particularly true in this marriage, where it would no longer be a question of building a family, or having a child, but only of a couple relationship, through which Mrs M. could find happiness again, and thus counteract the sanction that is inflicted on her.

7.2.3 Discussion

a. Body and Self-Representation

For Mrs A. and Mrs M., we have seen how their representations of their body were affected by these operations. Both have been feeling the pain of being dispossessed of an essential part of themselves. Their body image was disrupted, and this influenced their self-representation.

The Ego-Skin is based on a construction where mothering gave meaning to sensations, and distributed the libido in the body, after the primary seduction. This contributes to building an image mirrored by the Maternal Other and aiming toward an ideal pressured by its archaic superego. The woman builds herself as lacking, compared to Others who are whole. This lack is to be filled with alterity and is an endless patchwork. Therefore, as Eugénie Lemoine-Luccioni (1976) claims, the woman experiences partition or is divided:

> This other—which is not necessarily an object (a)—, the woman has no difficulty in recognizing it, when she finds it, because it was already there, constitutively. When, under the species of the penis or of the child that moves in her, of their own movement, it reappears, she separates herself from the imaginary other that has become useless as she will separate herself, when the time comes, from the penis and from the child. Rather than the anguish of castration, the woman thus feels the anguish of partition. She really lives under the sign of the abandonment: mother, father, children, husband, penis, everybody leaves her. (p. 71)[3]

This lack, imprinted on the body, is reactivated by the reality of the operation, where she experiences castration, before symbolically assumed

[3]Translated from original quote in French: "Cet autre—qui n'est pas pour autant objet (a)—, la femme n'a aucune peine à le reconnaitre, quand elle le trouve, parce qu'il était déjà là, constitutivement. Quand, sous les espèces du pénis ou de l'enfant qui bougent en elle, de leur propre mouvement, il réapparaît, elle se sépare de l'autre imaginaire devenu inutile comme elle se séparera, le moment venu, du pénis et de l'enfant. Plutôt que l'angoisse de la castration, la femme connaît ainsi l'angoisse de la partition. Elle vit vraiment sous le signe de l'abandon: mère, père, enfants, mari, pénis, tout le monde la quitte."

under the sign of "partition" as the author calls it. In the case of Mrs M., the scar is experienced as a narcissistic wound showing the reality of this loss.

b. Society and the Other

Both of our participants have described how the operation changed their relationship with their environment. Mrs A. has gained the prestige she wanted, and it has given her strength in her relationship with her husband. Whereas Mrs M. has felt the need to return to her parents and spend more time at their home. She has diminished the time she spends with others and is suspicious of their glances. The example of her niece who has seen her naked, or the perspective of being intimate with a new husband, shows the vulnerability she has with this lacking body, in society. She appears overtly diminished and feels the need to adapt to this new situation.

Mrs A. and Mrs M. mentioned the malevolence of other women as a potential source for their bad luck and the disease. Thus, other women are reflecting the Maternal Other's aggression and they must protect themselves against them, by rallying to religion, as protective. Both have used it as a coping mechanism and are empowered by its explanations. For Mrs A., her spiritual guide is an ally that figuratively represents the port where she takes refuge. The ambivalence between versions of womanhood is implied in both of their testimonies, only to seek causes of their dissatisfaction at the present time. Emancipation is valued in both testimonies but in different ways. Mrs A. seeks it because she needs to proceed with her self-reconstruction, and her position of prestige must be developed through this evolution. Mrs M. has always been emancipated but is turning toward her family for emotional support and energy to go forward with this reconstruction, as this experience has emphasized her loneliness.

Their position toward society is interesting as they were remarkably able to adapt and move on the social spectrum, seeking and finding what they needed to grow stronger. Their participation in this research shows that they know how important their experience is, as is their will to share it for others to understand.

c. Adornment and Masquerade

Mrs M.'s testimony has illustrated how her former position of superiority is challenged by this situation. Being in need is not something she is used to, as she has always been in a position of leadership in her family. This illusory phallus was balanced with a position of infantilization, where she remained her parents' little girl. This example is similar to Joan Riviere's patient because they developed the same pattern of showing coquetry and sensitivity to masculine approbation.

Her act of giving away her beautiful clothes to her nieces, and adopting a more sober style and a headscarf, shows that she is renouncing that part of herself that has enjoyed being watched.

Eugénie Lemoine-Luccioni has worked on the concept of the scopic impulse:

> The process is engaged from the moment when, operating the cut during the scopic impulse which governs her since always, the girl gives herself to be seen, instead of losing herself in the mirror. She then offers herself as object (a) and provokes the response of the Other, avoiding alienating identification. 'the incursion in the field of the Other' by provocation opens to her then the access to the symbolic/real register. In this 'giving to see', the scopic impulse proper to the woman makes her find her status of subject, since it is by this partial impulse that she manifests her desire of the Other and that she reaches him. After the encounter, something is changed, since the woman knows that what she wanted to see was the Other, the man as subject; and that what he wanted to know was the woman as point of origin, beyond the masquerade. (p. 87)[4]

[4] Translated from original quote in French: "Le processus est engagé dès l'instant où, opérant la coupure dans le parcours de la pulsion scopique qui la gouverne depuis toujours, la fille se donne à voir, au lieu de se perdre dans le miroir. Elle s'offre alors comme objet (a) et provoque la réponse de l'Autre, évitant l'identification aliénante. 'L'incursion au champ de l'Autre' par provocation lui ouvre alors l'accès au registre symbolique/réel. Dans ce 'donner à voir', la pulsion scopique propre à la femme lui fait trouver son statut de sujet, puisque c'est par cette pulsion partielle qu'elle manifeste son désir de l'Autre et qu'elle l'atteint. Après la rencontre, quelque chose est changé, puisque la femme sait que ce qu'elle voulait voir c'était l'Autre, l'homme en tant que sujet; et que ce qu'il voulait connaitre, lui, c'était la femme en tant que point d'origine, au-delà de la mascarade."

Thus Mrs M. has always been working on her image, as the object of attention, putting her efforts into her appearance. When she is seen by the head nurse (C.), she is revived and makes an effort to maintain her image. The headscarf, which she must wear to hide her new appearance, is described as cumbersome, and prevents her from gaining the attention she is used to. She is the chief of her family, but never fully acknowledges it, mentioning her brother as the most intellectual in the group. Her adornment represents her way of existing in society as a woman challenging men's positions.

Regarding Mrs A., adornment is a salvation, because it helps her build her femininity again when she must evolve to a new conception of maternity. She wants emancipation to be able to develop her adornment and needs that development to grow in her construction as a leader. This masquerade formed through her new appearance is healing, because it masks the lack, creates a substantial form, and attracts desire. As a leader in her community, she finally gets to the other jouissance.

In the previous chapters of this book, we discussed adornment reflecting social status, and we can see in our participants' histories how social hierarchy is also called into question. When Mrs A. changes status to become *Hadja* and earns the position of older sister in her family, she gains a higher hierarchical status in society. Her adornment must evolve to be consistent with this title, and her ambition to "dress properly" addresses this gap between financial dependency and higher social status. The masquerade operates at two levels in her life:

- Before the operation, she attributed a lot of importance to her husband's satisfaction and was more docile and compliant. She was in an accepted status of lack, and her masquerade was targeting her husband. Her dress code and attitude aimed to keep him satisfied and avoid his suspicion.
- Since the operation, the audience has changed for her, she no longer lives for him, but for her community, and herself. Her dress code and attitude aim to hide this lack and reflect the strength she has built. Her psychological reconstruction has led her to find new fillers for this

lack, and through them, she can feel the other jouissance. Her masquerade aims at those relays (social circle, daughter, spiritual guide), because they are the ones she is now interested in for her audience, and their desire is to see her as strong and independent.

d. Maternal Other versus Great Other

In this chapter, we have observed our participants' positions. They came from completely different environments and families. However, they are from the same country and share the same culture.

Mrs M. is still in a filial relationship with her parents, who she takes care of. Although they are a source of support and affection for her, she seems to have inverted the relationship, and she is in a parental position with them because she preserves them from knowing about her situation and takes care of them. She has reported staying very close with them, as she goes to their home on a regular basis. She attributes high importance to people with higher intellectual and professional status and has little respect for her female colleagues who disseminated her health information. It seems like the latter represent basic noxious women, relaying images of the Maternal Other, while more intellectual people reflect closer connection with the Great Other, present in her interaction with God, in the religious field.

Nevertheless, this dichotomy does not seem to be consistent, as in her relationship with religion there seem to also be a parameter of an aggressive maternal superego, destructive and destructuring. The same is to be noted in her relationship with her parents appearing as combined and never mentioned separately, pushing away the idea of triangulation. Therefore, it seems like she has invested religion as a third party, and that it combines the Others as a global superego. The ambivalence between femininity and maternity appears in the nuance of her navigation, and through her adornment. On the one hand, she was seductive and sexually attractive on the feminine side, and on the other she is austere and keen to sacrifice on the maternal side.

Regarding Mrs A., her relationship with her husband was not her only concern, as she mentioned the hardship of her global family situation. The Maternal Other appears through the pressure for her to give in to sacrifice. She has access to the spiritual guide as an ally, even in her marriage, and the doctor also plays this role. It seems like there is no one in her family who has played this role for her, and she was exposed to her husband before finding those allies. They represent the Great Other, and she embraces the religious knowledge, as a second attempt to gain this position, after her request to work in the medical field was rejected. Julia Kristeva (2000) has claimed that the first husband a woman chooses usually reflects the relationship she has with her mother. Mrs A.'s situation seems to illustrate this point, as it repeats this symbolic castration leaving her in the status of a subject aspiring to be completed through his satisfaction, and only gaining hers in this process. This operation allows her to see another destination for her desire, and she invests in religion as a space of accomplishment and becoming. There, the Great Other is the one granting jouissance and looking at her image. Women who are looking at her are finally seeing her as an ideal womanly version of femininity, and there she incarnates this Maternal Other on her own terms. In this perspective, she has incarnated both figures, showing that as much as the woman can be both maternal and feminine, Others are a combination of the Maternal Other and the Great Other.

The ambivalence of femininity lies in the fact that women combine those figures, as they are creators and creation, source and object of desire.

References

Diop, I. (2012). *Hystérectomy, mastectomie et statut de la femme au Sénégal* (Doctoral thesis, Université de Rouen, France).

Kristeva, J. (2000). *Le génie féminin*, 2. Mélanie Klein. Folio Essais.

Lemoine-Luccioni, E. (1976). *Partage des femmes*. Éditions du Seuil.

8

Conclusion

In the six chapters of this book, we have had the opportunity to address the topic of adornment and femininity in Africa, and how it reflects the masquerade of womanliness. The analysis of two clinical cases has allowed us to show how the participants' experiences have implied a change in their adornment after critical intervention challenged the symbolic basis of their womanhood.

We have discussed how adornment not only reflected social status but also political, cultural, and religious positions. Women, through their physical appearance, try as much as possible to gain control of their image and choose how they want to be seen. Although the codes of beauty have been inflicted on them and dictated by Eurocentric and androcentric views in a globalized dimension, African women still have their part to play, to retain their plural singularities in the world. We have seen the consequences of this globalization on the Ego-Skin, where transgenerational traumas connected to the time of slavery and then colonialism still cause insecurities and narcissistic wounds. The social reconstruction of black femininity is an effort to counter those traumas, but the work to reinforce self-esteem and value black identity is still in progress.

I. S. Diop, *Adornment, Masquerade and African Femininity*, Pan-African Psychologies,
https://doi.org/10.1007/978-3-031-28748-0_8

The analysis of our clinical cases shows how adornment also plays a role in women's social representations as members of the society's hierarchy, as our participants express how relevant it is in their professional and religious situation. Here we found again the representation of adornment as connected to the feminine ambivalence and masquerade femininity.

As a result of our reflection, we come to acknowledge the fact that the figures of the Maternal Other and the Great Other are ambivalent but complementary sides of the same entity. Women are at their intersection. Their status as objects of desire is a stage of their evolution, until they get beyond the Other's desire to chase their own: desiring themselves as powerful beings. This is the way to attain other jouissance, for longer than the short period of time when they are allowed to make the most of their fusional relationship with their newborn. Then, culture plays its role as regulator and symbolically castrates them in an infinite loop of castration-reconstruction, just like the moon cycle. Masquerade takes place to offer an attractive vision of a constantly approachable lacking and vulnerable subject to avoid inspiring anxiety in society. The scopic impulse pushes women to search for the other's gaze as fuel for their narcissism, until they finally get to see themselves in the mirror and are satisfied with this image as enviable.

In our previous book we asked the eternal question: What do women want? In this second book we may finally offer an answer: everything. They want to be seen, to choose who sees them and what to show. They want to see themselves and feel whole, to experience the same jouissance that others may feel when seeing them.

Attaining this level is the true emancipation, detached from calculations of financial and social acquisitions.

When analyzing our participants' comments, we found that they both had a significant relationship with their brothers, and one of them was considered worthy enough to be required for support. This has led us to introduce the question of the fraternal relationship, as founding and significative in the individual's construction. The brother is another mirror, as he is a compromising figure on the path to the father and is of the same generation. In African matriarchal societies, the place given to the maternal uncle further underlines this special relationship. The horizontal distribution already in place in several African cultures associated with the participation of peers in early education facilitates this diffraction of impulses. The relation between brother and sister is at the center of many projections, and we have found that many of our clinical situations that addressed the concept of *rabs*[1] had an implicit conflict related to the loss of a sibling before the patient's birth or in their early childhood.

In our next study, we aim to further observe this problematic. Indeed, this will allow us to continue this reflection on the mirror as point of self-revelation, because the manifestation of the *rab* could be connected to this scopic impulse, and the double image of the same, seen in the other.

[1] *Rab* is a wolof word designing a spirit that connects itself to a lineage and chooses someone with whom to form a bond, rejecting their environment and especially their partners. They manifest through psychosomatic symptoms and sometimes erotic dreams by their carrier. The *rab* is seen as being responsible of their mate's instability and/or incapacity to maintain a romantic relationship.

Index

I. S. Diop, *Adornment, Masquerade and African Femininity*, Pan-African Psychologies,
https://doi.org/10.1007/978-3-031-28748-0

The manufacturer's authorised representative in the EU is Springer Nature Customer Service Centre GmbH, Europaplatz 3, 69115 Heidelberg, Germany. If you have any concerns regarding our products, please contact ProductSafety@springernature.com

Printed and bound by CPI Group (UK) Ltd, Croydon, CR0 4YY
30/09/2026
02225311-0001